Subversive Sublimities

Subversive Sublimities: Undercurrents of the German Enlightenment

Edited by
Eitel Timm

CAMDEN HOUSE

Copyright © 1992 by
CAMDEN HOUSE, INC.

Published by Camden House, Inc.
Drawer 2025
Columbia, SC 29202 USA

Printed on acid-free paper.
Binding materials are chosen for strength and
durability.

All Rights Reserved
Printed in the United States of America
First Edition

Printed by Thomson-Shore Inc.
Dexter, Michigan

ISBN:1-879751-28-3

Library of Congress Cataloging-in-Publication Data

Subversive sublimities : undercurrents of the German Enlightenment /
edited by Eitel Timm. -- 1st ed.
    p.   cm. -- (Studies in German literature, linguistics, and culture)
    Includes bibliographical references and index.
    ISBN 1-879751-28-3 (alk. paper)
    1. German literature--18th century--History and criticism.
2. Enlightenment--Germany. I. Timm, Eitel Friedrich. II. Series:
Studies in German literature, linguistics, and culture (Unnumbered)
PT285.S8 1992
830.9'006--dc20   92-17546
                                                                            CIP

Contents

EITEL TIMM, *University of British Columbia, Vancouver*
Introductory Notes   vii

DENNIS F. MAHONEY, *University of Vermont, Burlington*
Human History as Natural History
in *Die Lehrlinge zu Sais* and *Heinrich von Ofterdingen*   1

ARND BOHM, *Carleton University, Ottawa*
The Desublimated Body: Gottfried August Bürger   12

WANDA VAN DUSEN, *University of California, San Diego*
Reconciling Reason with Sensibility: Jakob Michael Reinhold
Lenz's *Anmerkungen übers Theater*   27

WULF KOEPKE, *Texas A&M University, College Station*
The Devil and Aesthetic Nihilism   36

THOMAS SALUMETS, *University of British Columbia, Vancouver*
Pleasures of Influence: Goethe, Bloom, Elias   45

PRISCILLA HAYDEN-ROY, *University of Nebraska, Lincoln*
Sensate Language and the Hermetic Tradition in Friedrich
Christoph Oetinger's *Biblisches und Emblematisches Wörterbuch*   58

CHARLOTTE M. CRAIG, *Kutztown University, Pennsylvania*
Nicolai and the Occult   70

EDWARD DIXON, *Swarthmore College, Pennsylvania*
Reason in Revolt — Christian Heinrich Spieß
and the *Tales of Insanity*   76

ANNE LEBLANS, *St. Mary's College, Maryland*
Kinder- und Hausmärchen: The Creation of Male Wombs
as a Means of Protection against the Fear of Engulfment   86

CHRISTIANE STANINGER, *University of California, San Diego*
E.T.A. Hoffmann's *Der Sandmann* as Critique of
the Enlightenment   98

WILLIAM CRISMAN, *Penn State University, Altoona*
"Ohne alle Überzeugung überzeugt zu tun":
Masonic Voodoo in the Young Tieck's Enlightenment Novels   105

INDEX   115

Eitel Timm

Introductory Notes

MASSIVE SHIFTS IN THE FORMS OF THOUGHT and life in the Age of the German Enlightenment have led to the widely accepted dictum that the manifold transitions in the late eighteenth and early nineteenth centuries were elements of a gradual formation of intellectual and aesthetic modernity. The idea of imperceptible progress, which was perhaps the most decisive shaping force of Western Judeo-Christian culture, unswervingly outlived the turmoil of fundamental challenges to traditional values. Under the obligation of a homogeneous and ideologically dominant programme phenomena such as esoteric thought, occultism, shamanism, mesmerism, etc, in short: irrational perceptions of world and self were relegated to the sphere of not yet enlightened historical relics. Flourishing secret societies as well as the challenges of early European Romanticism, however, denote substantial deficiencies with regard to intellectual responses of proponents of modernity's adamant paradigm. It has become almost a doctrine of Enlightenment critique that Romanticism propagated precepts of thought consisting of interactive principles which have thus shaped our sense of modernity.[1] But these pretensions to hermeneutic unity of understanding have a tendency to obliterate unsurmountable differences between aesthetic affirmation and revolt. Kant's conspicuous hysteria in view of the dispute with Swedenborg is perhaps one of the most significant indications of the inherent threats posed by — what were from within the frame of the constitutionalized system nonetheless — undomesticated, dark forces.[2] It is no exaggeration to say that the Age of Enlightenment is un-

---

[1] Cf. Ernst Behler, "Infinite Perfectibility. European Romanticism and the French Revolution," in: *The French Revolution and the Age of Goethe*, ed. Gerhart Hoffmeister, (Hildesheim: Olms, 1989), p. 126; Behler argues that "the particular style of this new type of discourse seems to consist in the movement of several counteractive principles (affirmation and scepticism, enthusiasm and melancholy) which seem to negate, but in their interaction maintain one another."

[2] More explicitly ideological were, for example, contemporary accounts of mesmerist activities in France. Suspected of a secret, subversive, and conspiratorial agenda, radical political thinkers and philosophers attempted quite eagerly to appropriate mesmeric practices for their critique of the Enlightenment. Cf. Robert Darnton, *Mesmerism and the End of the Enlightenment in France*, (Cambridge, Mass.: Harvard University Press, 1968), p. 79 et passim. It is interesting to note that when Fichte in 1813 reflected on the scope of his system of natural sciences he unabashedly contemplated the theoretical and practical challenges of animal magnetism. Cf. Johann Gottlieb Fichte, *Nachgelassene Werke*, (Bonn, 1835), vol. III, p. 311.

intelligible except in relation to the modes in which this dark side manifests itself in aesthetic expression and socio-cultural objectivations.

On the present threshold of a deliberate emancipation from homogenetic explanatory paradigms critical orientation requires perhaps new, autonomous epistemological configurations. If, therefore, the axiomatic propositions of enlightened thought were taken out of the traditional prescriptive hermeneutic context, the field of critical inquiry would be prepared for a radical shift from interpretation to exegesis: the "rage of [unifying] understanding"[3] would make way for a process in which the original text surfaces as text in clear. What in modern critical thought appear to be undercurrents of German Enlightenment could then emerge as phenomena which read as generic documents rather than concomitant texts requiring reevaluating subtextual explanation. The sublime perceptive quality of most of the texts investigated in this study come to the fore not despite their subversive resistance to dialectical analysis but because of the inherent aesthetically insurgent potential.

When under the influence of *Naturphilosophie* the rise of the two cultures (empirical science and humanities) became the hallmark of modernity,[4] the subversive potential of Enlightenment critique shifted from the objective realm of natural phenomena (such as magnetism, mineralogy etc) to subjective artistic representations of world and self.[5] At this juncture of modern history, however, it became apparent that the forces undermining the project of modernity could not be relegated to the ensuing secondary culture. The metaphoricity of modern science has largely sustained linguistic systems as aspects of its methodology.[6] What appears to be general modern scepticism with regard to cognitive theories of metaphor seems to possess a more universal quality as a *weltanschauung* and, perhaps, protoreligion irreverent of the domineering power of unifying explanatory systems.

Since the focus of this publication is intentionally on discontinuities and heterogeneity, on the marginal rather than the canon, it may also be seen as a contribution to the gradual formation of new approaches to the writing of literary history. If the so-called historical background becomes an integral element of what Derrida designates as "le text général," the textuality of history necessarily entails the depriveleging of the authority of canonized literary texts. Walter Benjamin's

---

[3] Jochen Hörisch, *Die Wut des Verstehens*, (Frankfurt: Suhrkamp,1988), p. 51f.

[4] C.P. Snow, *The Two Cultures and a Second Look*, (Cambridge, 1969).

[5] Cf. Walter Wetzels, *Johann Wilhelm Ritter: Physik im Wirkungsfeld der deutschen Romantik*, (Berlin, 1973), p. 88ff.

[6] C.f. David Porush, "Endoxical Discourse: A Post-modern Model for the Relation between Science and Literature," *Modern Language Studies*, XX, 4, (Fall, 1990), 59ff.

concept of a "montage of history"[7] necessitates a reorganizing of the material for investigation: surfacing in such a manner "subversive sublimities" may then perhaps indeed "create [through a new historicism] a critical situation for the present."[8]

The book was conceived as a proliferation of thoughts originating in general contemporary concern over consolidating hermeneutic concepts which have shaped the modern critics' values with regard to interpretation and reading of enlightenment texts. The choice of topics in this study hopefully provides also sufficient evidence for the legitimacy of one of the underlying questions raised — in various forms — in the individual articles: Is not the dark side of the Enlightenment less a relic of past unenlightened anthropological periods but rather a blunt expression of fundamental opposition to the project of modernity?

---

[7] Walter Benjamin, *Das Passagen-Werk*, ed. Rolf Tiedemann, (Frankfurt: Suhrkamp, 1983), vol I, p. 575. Cf. also: Rainer Nägele, *Benjamin's Ground: New Readings of Walter Benjamin*, (Detroit: Wayne State University Press, 1988), Introduction.

[8] Ibidem, p. 588.

Dennis F. Mahoney

Human History as Natural History in *Die Lehrlinge zu Sais* and *Heinrich von Ofterdingen*

IN HIS ARTICLE ON "New Historicism and the Study of German Literature," Anton Kaes articulates a position that can be of help as we undertake a fresh look at Novalis, the late eighteenth century, and indeed other writers, writings, and historical periods:

> All cultural production has a social dimension: it articulates what a society lacks and desires. It delivers in the make-believe world of fiction what cannot be had or said in reality. In order to reactivate this social dimension of a literary text, one must reconstruct the question(s) that the work answers and addresses. The classical works of German literature in particular need to be understood once again as answers to questions that have their basis in the material as well as the ideological world.[1]

To this critical insight must be added the reminder that the questions we ask are themselves triggered by areas in the text that address, challenge, or otherwise activate our own present concerns and our goals for the future. In this respect, the "utility" of texts like *Die Lehrlinge zu Sais* and *Heinrich von Ofterdingen* is to be measured less by the answers they provide than by the questions they continue to elicit from their readers.

Proceeding from these suppositions, I intend to investigate Novalis's deliberate evocation of attitudes towards nature earlier than and different from those prevailing in the science of his day and age. At the same time as he was studying the latest developments in chemistry and geology at the Mining Academy of Freiberg in 1798 and 1799, in works such as *Die Lehrlinge zu Sais* and *Heinrich von Ofterdingen* he chose settings distant in time and space as well as vitalistic notions of nature reminiscent of the alchemists of medieval Europe, with the image of nature as the goddess Isis extending back even further into human memory. Protesting

---

[1] Anton Kaes, "New Historicism and the Study of German Literature," *German Quarterly* 62 (1989), p. 215. For further information on the lively debates concerning this new direction in literary studies, cf. the lengthy documentation provided by Kaes at the conclusion of his article (216–219) and also the anthology *The New Historicism*, ed. H. Aram Veeser (London, New York: Routledge, 1989).

against an instrumentalist use of reason that ultimately estranges humans from themselves as well as their natural surroundings, Novalis chose to emphasize the bonds of love linking together all living creatures. At the same time he also advocated an envisioned "moralization of nature," whereby the world is enhanced and beautified through human work. Thus Novalis makes use of a mystical Egyptian temple and a poeticized Middle Ages as models of a mutually enriching interaction between humanity and nature still to be realized in the Europe of his own day. By extending the Romantic continuum of reflection into our own time we in turn can examine to what extent these ideas of Novalis have a place in our own ecologically conscious world, where the eighteenth-century pride in becoming the masters of our own destinies has been supplanted by the knowledge that we humans can also easily become the sources of global destruction as well.

In a letter to Ludwig Tieck dated September 20, 1802, thanking him for having located a missing manuscript for the planned second volume of Novalis's works, August Wilhelm Schlegel wrote: "Den wiedergefundenen Aufsatz von Hardenberg haben wir alle mit großem Entzücken gelesen, es ist ein herrliches und vielleicht sein eigenthümlichstes Werk."[2] That one of the founding members of German Early Romanticism would describe *Die Lehrlinge zu Sais* as being an essay itself indicates the novelty of the blending of poetry, philosophy and rhetoric called for in Friedrich Schlegel's 116th *Athenäum*-Fragment and put into practice by Novalis in the *Lehrlinge*. As the title of the work might have led an early reader to expect a novel in the tradition of Goethe's *Wilhelm Meisters Lehrjahre*, it is instructive to compare the beginnings of these two works. Goethe's first chapter opens with the words "Das Schauspiel dauerte sehr lange"[3] and leads quickly to Wilhelm's tryst with his lover Mariane. The *Lehrlinge*, on the other hand, begins with the following reflections:

> Mannichfache Wege gehen die Menschen. Wer sie verfolgt und vergleicht, wird wunderliche Figuren entstehen sehn; Figuren, die zu jener großen Chiffernschrift zu gehören scheinen, die man überall, auf Flügeln, Eierschalen, in Wolken, im Schnee, in Krystallen und in Steinbildungen, auf gefrierenden Wassern, im Innern und Äußern der Gebirge, der Pflanzen, der Thiere, der Menschen, in den Lichtern des Himmels, auf berührten und gestrichenen Scheiben von Pech und Glas, in den Feilspänen um den Magnet her, und sonderbaren Conjuncturen des Zufalls, erblickt (I: 79).

Written during his studies at the Mining Academy of Freiberg — the prosaic equivalent of the Egyptian temple of Sais mentioned in the text — and the product of his extensive readings in natural science and idealistic philosophy, Novalis's *Die*

---

[2] References to Novalis's works are taken from the historical-critical edition of Novalis, *Schriften*, (Stuttgart: Kohlhammer, 1960 ff.; quotes from volume I refer to the 1977 revised edition) and henceforth will be listed parenthetically in the main text. This quote, for example, would be listed according to volume and page number as follows: (V: 153).

[3] Goethe, *Wilhelm Meisters Lehrjahre*, in *Werke*, (München: Beck, 1973) VII: 9.

Lehrlinge zu Sais is an example of the transference of material from different discourses into the aesthetic realm that has become a focus of New Historicist studies. While the tone of these opening words might indeed suggest an "essay," both the rhythm of the language and the reference to a code, or "Chiffernschrift," throughout nature seem inappropriate for normal scientific writing, putting the reader into a state of uncertainty calculated to cause him or her to reconsider past attitudes towards nature. In an adaptation of the image of nature being a book written by God, the varied paths taken by people are seen as part of the "Wunderschrift" (I: 79) evident throughout all of nature. Indeed, they are surmised to be the key to deciphering the hidden message, a notion also expressed in the main image of the *Lehrlinge*: the unveiling of the goddess Isis. Novalis's apprentice ends the first chapter of this work with the resolve: "Auch ich will also meine Figur beschreiben, und wenn kein Sterblicher, nach jener Inschrift dort, den Schleyer hebt, so müssen wir Unsterbliche zu werden suchen; wer ihn nicht heben will, ist kein ächter Lehrling zu Sais" (I: 82).

Rather than plot narration, though, one encounters in the *Lehrlinge* an array of conversations and reflections. The lifting of the veil of Isis, for example, does not occur in the depiction of the apprentice's own activities, but rather in the conclusion to the fairy tale of "Hyazinth und Rosenblütchen" (I: 91-95). Prior to the telling of this tale, the apprentice had been dismayed by a series of conflicting accounts of the essence of nature; for some nature was "eine furchtbare Mühle des Todes" (I: 88), for others an enemy to be conquered, for still others the object of introspective contemplation or ethical activism. Most commentators understand this latter position to be a reflection of Fichtean philosophy, as when "ein ernster Mann" states: "Die Andern reden irre [...]. Erkennen sie in der Natur nicht den treuen Abdruck ihrer selbst?" (I: 90). But it is significant that even this mode of argumentation is depicted as adding to the trepidation of the apprentice rather than alleviating it (I, 91); only the fairy tale frees him from his self-imposed isolation and provides him with that same sense of love for nature attained by Hyazinth after a long and arduous journey. In similar fashion, we readers of the *Lehrlinge* are expected to internalize the insights gained by the apprentice and to synthesize the messages of the other conversations subsequent to the fairy tale, which culminate in the proclamation of love and poetry as the keys of access to nature.[4]

Indeed, it is the fairy tale — a genre explicitly set in the world of fantasy and make-believe — that appears to initiate a magical transformation among the collection of objects arranged within the temple of Sais in the manner of eighteenth-century mineral cabinets. Once the apprentice and his tale-telling companion have embraced and departed, the following conversation ensues:

---

[4] Cf. the chapter "Das Gespräch der Reisenden" in: Dennis F. Mahoney, *Die Poetisierung der Natur bei Novalis. Beweggründe, Gestaltung, Folgen*, (Bonn: Bouvier, 1980), p. 38-52.

> O! daß der Mensch, sagten sie, die innre Musik der Natur verstände, und einen Sinn für äußere Harmonie hätte. Aber er weiß ja kaum, daß wir zusammen gehören, und keins ohne das andere bestehen kann. Er kann nichts liegen lassen, tyrannisch trennt er uns und greift in lauter Dissonanzen herum. Wie glücklich könnte er seyn, wenn er mit uns freundlich umginge, und auch in unserm großen Bund träte, wie ehemals in der goldnen Zeit, wie er sie mit Recht nennt (I: 95).

By providing a subjectivity — "wir" — to what are generally perceived as *objects*, Novalis suggests an aesthetic solution to the binary separation between "Man" and "Nature" that produces a reified world for us all, as well as a return to a hypothetically primeval Golden Age.

At this point it might be worthwhile to consider why such wishes are being articulated. Novalis generally is credited with the creation of the verb "romantisieren." Jurij Striedter, in his analysis of the opening paragraphs of the *Lehrlinge*, has demonstrated how Novalis, by simultaneously making the abstract concrete and providing a universal significance for individual phenomena, has put into practice his postulate "Die Welt muß romantisirt werden" (II: 545).[5] The notebook entry immediately preceding Novalis's call for the romanticization of the world makes explicit the reason and the need for such a program: "Ehemals war alles Geistererscheinung. Jezt sehn wir nichts, als todte Wiederholung, die wir nicht verstehn. Die Bedeutung der Hieroglyfe fehlt. Wir leben noch von der Frucht besserer Zeiten" (II: 545). This idea of dead repetition — reminiscent of Schiller's image in *Die Götter Griechenlands* of the "toten Schlag der Pendeluhr" in a world seen as governed by mechanistic principles[6] — is assailed in a speech by one of the travelers to Sais in the *Lehrlinge*, who decries how nature has been reduced "zur einförmigen Maschine, ohne Vorzeit und Zukunft" (I: 99). Thanks to his geological studies in Freiberg, Novalis had the opportunity to familiarize himself with the first modern science to concern itself with natural *history*. In addition, the ancient German mining traditions, which held that minerals actually grew underground,[7] provided a counterbalance to the notion of inanimate nature predominant in Western science and philosophy since Descartes, through which nature had come to be viewed as manipulable by human beings understanding themselves as pure disembodied intelligence. Theodore Ziolkowski has pointed out that, whereas in late eighteenth-century England mining had already become a key element in the industrial revolution and mines themselves had acquired the image of being dark, dangerous, and disagreeable places, in Germany the efforts of poet-scientists such as Novalis led to mines becoming not only favored sites for excursions but

---

[5] Jurij Striedter, *Die Fragmente des Novalis als "Präfiguration" seiner Dichtung*, (München: Fink, 1985), p. 156–162.

[6] Cf. Schiller, *Werke*, (München: Hanser, 1960), Vol I, p. 168.

[7] Cf. Theodore Ziolkowski, *German Romanticism and its Institutions*, (Princeton: Princeton UP, 1990), p. 29–30.

also images for the descent into the recesses of the human psyche, including sexuality.[8] For Novalis it is love by which we learn most about nature and ourselves, and thereby become equipped with the means to transform the earth back into the paradise it was meant to be. In his fairy tale within the *Lehrlinge*, and then again in the narrative framework of *Heinrich von Ofterdingen*, Novalis depicts such a process of loving as learning, in the hope that this make-believe construct would make such a belief come true for his readers as well.

Although a first reading of *Heinrich von Ofterdingen* would suggest a glorification of the Middle Ages as already being a Golden Age, it is significant that at the beginning of this novel its main character is already recalling a tale of former times "wie da die Thiere und Bäume und Felsen mit den Menschen gesprochen hätten" (I: 195) and that Heinrich's father dismisses the import of his dream of the Blue Flower by asserting: "In dem Alter der Welt, wo wir leben, findet der unmittelbare Verkehr mit dem Himmel nicht mehr statt" (I: 198).[9] In a framework typical of idealistic *Geschichtsphilosophie* Novalis is positing in his novel a "Middle Ages" set apart from an initial naive union between humanity and nature but yet also suggesting signs of a reunion between the two on a higher plane.

In her conversation with Heinrich in chapter 4 of the novel, the Saracen maiden Zulima interprets the destructive onslaught of the Christian crusaders as an unconscious, albeit destructive impulse to return to what she describes as the ancestral home of the human race:

> Das Leben auf einem längst bewohnten und ehemals schon durch Fleiß, Thätigkeit und Neigung verherrlichten Boden hat einen besondern Reiz. Die Natur scheint dort menschlicher und verständlicher geworden, eine dunkle Erinnerung unter der durchsichtigen Gegenwart wirft die Bilder der Welt mit scharfen Umrissen zurück, und so genießt man eine doppelte Welt, die eben dadurch das Schwere und Gewaltsame verliert und die zauberische Dichtung und Fabel unserer Sinne wird. Wer weiß, ob nicht auch ein unbegreiflicher Einfluß der ehemaligen, jetzt unsichtbaren Bewohner mit ins Spiel kommt, und vielleicht ist es dieser dunkle Zug, der die Menschen aus neuen Gegenden, sobald eine gewisse Zeit ihres Erwachens kömmt, mit so zerstörender Ungeduld nach der alten Heymath ihres Geschlechts treibt, und sie Gut und Blut an den Besitz dieser Länder zu wagen anregt (I: 237).

Heinrich himself is almost persuaded to join the carousing Crusaders in their next campaign, but it is noteworthy that even before his conversation with Zulima, who

---

[8] Ziolkowski, op. cit., p. 23–28.

[9] Both Nicholas Saul, *History and Poetry in Novalis and the Tradition of the German Enlightenment*, (London: U of London, 1984), p. 172 and Friedrich Strack, *Im Schatten der Neugier. Christliche Tradition und kritische Philosophie im Werk Friedrichs von Hardenberg*, (Tübingen: Niemeyer, 1982), p. 22–23 interpret this conversation between father and son as indicative of late eighteenth-century debates on the possibility of revelation in a post-Biblical age.

enlightens him as to the base behavior of Christian "pilgrims" in Jerusalem,[10] Heinrich's enthusiasm for war becomes tempered by his contemplation of the vast expanses of nature outside the narrow confines of the dark and gloomy castle: Das kriegerische Getümmel verlor sich, und es blieb nur eine klare bilderreiche Sehnsucht zurück (I: 234).

In chapter 5 of the novel, the figure of the miner will make use of a similar movement from a confined area to a liberating walk through nature in order to dissuade his audience, the merchants and peasants, from thoughts of material gain (I: 251). It is during this moonlit walk that Heinrich experiences his first conscious apprehension of the fundamental unity in nature:

> Die Worte des Alten hatten eine versteckte Tapetenthür in ihm geöffnet. Er sah sein kleines Wohnzimmer dicht an einen erhabenen Münster gebaut, aus dessen steinernem Boden die ernste Vorwelt emporstieg, während von der Kuppel die klare frölische [sic] Zukunft in goldnen Engelskindern ihr singend entgegenschwebte. Gewaltige Klänge bebten in den silbernen Gesang, und zu den weiten Thoren traten alle Creaturen herein, von denen jede ihre innere Natur in einer einfachen Bitte und in einer eigenthümlichen Mundart vernehmlich aussprach. Wie wunderte er sich, daß ihm diese klare, seinem Daseyn schon unentbehrliche Ansicht so lange fremd geblieben war (I: 252).

This vision, situated in the exact center of the first half of the novel,[11] already provides an intimation that Heinrich's initial dream of communion and communication with nature is destined to be fulfilled in Part II of the novel, where even rocks, flowers, wind, and trees comfort Heinrich after the death of his beloved Mathilde. But it is also significant that Novalis chooses a human art — architecture — as here providing the image of the place of reconciliation: not a prelapsarian garden, but rather a cathedral as representative of a "New Jerusalem" on earth. In other words, human constructs can be used to cut people off from their environment and block out the light from outside, so to speak; or they can become cosmic temples encompassing past, present, future, and all creatures of the earth in one harmonious whole.

As the figure of the miner plays an immensely important role in Heinrich's development, we might do well to look at him more closely. Just as with the teacher in *Die Lehrlinge zu Sais*, this character provides clear evidence of the reverence Novalis felt for his professor of geology at the Mining Academy of Freiberg, Abraham Gottlob Werner, whose last name he bears (I: 243-244). The

---

[10] Cf. my discussion of this scene in *Ofterdingen* and its eighteenth-century context in "Stages in Enlightenment. Lessing's *Nathan der Weise* and Novalis's *Heinrich von Ofterdingen*," *Seminar* 23 (1987), p. 206–208.

[11] For the classic interpretation of this key scene in *Ofterdingen*, cf. Hans-Joachim Mähl, *Die Idee des goldenen Zeitalters im Werk des Novalis*, (Heidelberg: Winter, 1965), p. 420–422.

miner displays a very "modern" curiosity[12] in exploring the recesses of the earth, and he can only smile at the peasants' fantastic stories of dragons, monsters, ghosts, and robbers occasioned by the presence of large numbers of bones within nearby caves (I: 251). He himself willingly participates in the extraction of mineral ore and gems from within the earth, and expressly mentions how through the efforts of his father-in-law Bohemia has become a rich and prosperous land. But as modern a figure as the miner seems to be with respect to his knowledge and industriousness, so traditional is he in his attitude towards nature, which receives its most concentrated expression in a song he remembers from his youth:

Der ist der Herr der Erde,
Wer ihre Tiefen mißt,
Und jeglicher Beschwerde
In ihrem Schooß vergißt.

Wer ihrer Felsenglieder
Geheimen Bau versteht,
Und unverdrossen nieder
Zu ihrer Werkstatt geht.

Er ist mit ihr verbündet,
Und inniglich vertraut,
Und wird von ihr entzündet,
Als wär' sie seine Braut (I: 247).

Not only is the earth depicted as a living creature — a break with the division between mind and matter prominent in Western thought since Descartes — but is described in explicitly feminine terms, an outlook that Carolyn Merchant has explored in her book *The Death of Nature*.[13] Within Novalis's own writings, one sees parallels between this song's conflation of femininity and nature and the fairy tale in the *Lehrlinge*, where Hyazinth leaves behind his childhood sweetheart in search of the goddess Isis only to rediscover Rosenblüthchen behind the veil in the innermost sanctuary of the temple. According to Novalis, such an unveiling is possible because human beings are themselves part of nature — cf. the names Hyazinth and Rosenblüthchen — and therefore can enter into productive and loving discourse with the world around them. In his explicit rejection of Fichte's notion of the "Nichtich" Novalis had written "Statt Nichtich — Du" (III: 430), thereby advocating what we would nowadays call an "I — Thou" relationship not only among human beings but also with respect to our natural environment. And

---

[12] For the importance of curiosity for the understanding of Novalis, cf. Strack, *Im Schatten der Neugier*.

[13] Carolyn Merchant, *The Death of Nature. Ecology, Women, and the Scientific Revolution*, (San Francisco: Harper & Row, 1980). See also Horst Bredekamp, "Die Erde als Lebewesen," *Kritische Berichte* 9. 4/5 (1981), p. 5–37.

so the work of the miner is not a matter of exploiting the "natural resources" of a foreign and hostile element, but rather an opportunity for self-knowledge and for the appreciation of the natural and divine wonders above and beneath the ground. As Helmut Gold has demonstrated, for Novalis mining becomes an analogy for the practice of romantic art itself, where the amalgamation of old and new and the exploration of that which had previously been dark and inaccessible are to bring about an Enlightenment far transcending utilitarian goals.[14]

When exploring the caves under the guidance of the miner, Heinrich encounters not only a presentiment of his own life story in the manuscript of the hermit; he also receives a sense of the earth's history amidst the profusion of fossilized bones strewn throughout the subterranean passageways, and attentively listens to the conversation between the miner and the hermit on the interrelationship between human and natural history.[15] When contemplating the remnants of prehistoric times and imagining the tumultuous conditions that produced such monstrous creatures, floods, and cataclysms, the hermit seems to himself "wie ein Traum der Zukunft, wie ein Kind des ewigen Friedens" (I: 261). The miner, commenting on "jene allmählige Beruhigung der Natur" (I: 261), observes that while nature may have lost its generative energies from these former times, it has in turn become more refined and ennobled: "Sie nähert sich dem Menschen, und wenn sie ehmals ein wildgebährender Fels war, so ist sie jetzt eine stille, treibende Pflanze, eine stumme menschliche Künstlerinn" (I: 262). Seen in this light, human beings, rather than being radically different from a lifeless nature, are instead the hitherto ultimate example of the earth's creative processes, with the responsibility for continuing and guiding patterns inherent in the earth's development. Such a viewpoint makes it clear why even as a student, according to Friedrich Schlegel's letter of January 1792, the young Friedrich von Hardenberg was of the opinion that there was nothing evil in the world and that everything was nearing the Golden Age again. (IV: 572).

And yet in *Heinrich von Ofterdingen* nature is not praised in an unqualified way. Sylvester, Heinrich's mentor in morality, speaks of "Nachhalle der alten unmenschlichen Natur" that need to be supplanted by "weckende Stimmen der höhern Natur, des himmlischen Gewissens in uns" (I: 330). Likewise the poet Klingsohr instructs his young protegé about another, less poetic side of nature: "Es ist in ihr, wie in dem Menschen, ein entgegengesetztes Wesen, die dumpfe Begierde und die stumpfe Gefühllosigkeit und Trägheit, die einen rastlosen Streit

---

[14] Helmut Gold, *Erkenntnisse unter Tage. Bergbaumotive in der Literatur der Romantik*, (Opladen: Westdeutscher Verlag, 1990), esp. p. 56–106 and 201–233.

[15] Cf. Hartmut Böhme, "Montan-Bau und Berg-Geheimniß. Zum Verhältnis von Bergbauwissenschaft und hermetischer Naturästhetik bei Novalis" in: *Idealismus und Aufklärung. Kontinuität und Kritik der Aufklärung in Philosophie und Poesie um 1800*, ed. Christoph Jamme und Gerhard Kurz, (Stuttgart: Klett-Cotta, 1988), p. 59–79, esp. p. 75–78.

mit der Poesie führen. Er wäre ein schöner Stoff zu einem Gedicht, dieser gewaltige Kampf" (I: 284). The poem in question is in fact no other than the fairy tale Klingsohr tells later that evening, which culminates in the establishment of a kingdom of love and peace on earth, where Sophie (Wisdom — but also the name of Novalis's deceased fiancée Sophie von Kühn) is reunited with her husband Arktur, the king of stars and metals alike, and life is restored to the frozen realm of the North Pole.

This use of the genre of the fairy tale — along with the incorporation of characters such as Eros, from Apuleius's tale of Cupid and Psyche, and Freya, the Germanic goddess of Love — is meant to evoke memories of tales from the childhood of individuals as well as of cultures. At the same time, these characters are involved in a plot making extensive use of electromagnetic and other recently discovered natural phenomena; the light issuing forth from Freya seems to suggest the Northern Lights, for instance (I: 290–291), while it is the electrically charged iron sword splinter cast out into the world that serves to guide Eros to his goal of finding Freya (I: 293).[16] The scribe, meanwhile — the first to notice that this compass needle always points north — busies himself with an extensive account of "den Nutzen, den dieser Fund gewähren könne" (I: 295), but is vexed to learn that his entire writing fails to pass Wisdom's test and is erased completely. The real key to the significance of this find has been provided already by Arktur's instructions: "Es wird alles gut. Eisen, wirf du dein Schwerdt in die Welt, daß sie erfahren, wo der Friede ruht" (I: 293).

In a June 18, 1800 letter to Friedrich Schlegel providing some clues to the allegorical interpretation of this fairy tale, Novalis made reference to "der Petrificirende und Petrificirte Verstand" (IV: 333) — a remark generally applied to the figure of the scribe, who is then thought to represent the mechanistic, instrumental aspect of Enlightenment philosophy and science. Such an interpretation, while doubtless correct, also needs to include an appreciation of the personal mythology that Novalis has built into his tale. Novalis recognized the "scribe" as being very much a part of himself, as the following words from a letter immediately after the death of Sophie von Kühn indicate:

Weich geboren hat mein Verstand sich nach und nach ausgedehnt und unvermerkt das Herz aus seinen Besitzungen verdrängt. Sofie gab den Herzen den verlohrenen

---

[16] For interpretations of the scientific and meta-scientific components of the Klingsohr tale, cf. Walter Wetzels, "Klingsohrs Märchen als Science Fiction," *Monatshefte* 65 (1973), p. 167–175 and Frederick Burwick, *The Damnation of Newton. Goethe's Color Theory and Romantic Perception*, (Berlin, New York: de Gruyter, 1986), p. 102–138.

Tron wieder — Wie leicht könnte ihr Tod nicht dem Usurpator die Herrschaft wieder geben, der dann gewiß rächend das Herz vertilgen würde (IV: 215).[17]

Such a process is depicted in the Klingsohr tale, where the scribe and his minions use the absence of Eros from the house of the human spirit to burn the Mother at the stake; paradoxically enough, her death brings about the demise of their own reign as well, for her funeral pyre extinguishes the light of the sun and melts the ice of the long winter's night that had prevailed in the realm of nature (I: 307–308). Were one to interpret the Klingsohr tale as a prophetic document, as Novalis's theory of the fairy tale would have us do, the end of a falsely understood Enlightenment is being proclaimed, and with it the establishment of a new and greater Golden Age on earth. Nature, whom Novalis had described as a "versteinerte Zauberstadt" (III: 564) in a notebook entry of 1799, is to be freed from its magic spell through the agency of poetry (Fabel) and love (Eros). At the end of the fairy tale, the throne from which Eros and Freya are to reign is transformed into a "Hochzeitsbett" (I: 315) signifying the marriage of heaven and earth, while the scribe and his followers have been turned into "petrified" chess pieces, as symbolic representations of war, strife, and the "alten trüben Zeit" (I: 314) that will reign no more. If one recalls that the French Revolutionary Wars were raging throughout Europe at the time Novalis wrote his fairy tale, Anton Kaes's notion of literature articulating what a society lacks and desires takes on particular meaning.

When contemplating these visions from a perspective almost two hundred years after their publication, however, the apocalyptic overtones to Klingsohr's tale are not calculated to appeal to a world for which universal conflagration is no longer a mere metaphor.[18] Today we are likely to look askance at Novalis's feminization of nature, particularly as his gender-based narratives leave figures such as Rosenblüthchen and Freya the more or less passive objects of their lovers' quests, while the "Herr der Erde" perspective of the miner (I: 247) should caution against the overly hasty claiming of Novalis as a proto-feminist ecologist. And however appealing the romantic hope may be that behind the diverse phenomena there is an inherent meaning to nature capable of being made manifest by art, contemporary readers are more likely to respond to suggestions in Novalis's

---

[17] The editors of the historical-critical edition of the *Schriften* regard this passage from the letter of March 29, 1797 to Novalis's friend and Mentor Kreisamtmann Just as a "Vorklang auf Klingsohrs Märchen im 9. Kapitel des *Heinrich von Ofterdingen* (IV: 816)."

[18] Cf. Géza von Molnár's explication and critique of Heinrich's and Klingsohr's glorification of war in his penetrating study *Romantic Vision, Ethical Context. Novalis and Artistic Autonomy*, (Minneapolis: U of Minnesota P, 1987), p. 153–156.

private notebooks that it is we who arrange the "Weltchaos" (III: 179) into patterns of our own creation.[19]

In the end, it is by provoking such skeptical responses and encouraging us to articulate our own visions of a fruitful interplay between humanity and nature that *Die Lehrlinge zu Sais* and *Heinrich von Ofterdingen* maintain their freshness. One of the most congenial aspects of the early German romantics is that they expected their writings to be surpassed by their readers, just as they regard their criticism of and responses to such works as Goethe's *Wilhelm Meisters Lehrjahre* to be an advancement on the originals. In the *Lehrlinge*, as in *Ofterdingen*, there is no absolute authority; even the teacher acknowledges the superiority of a child (I: 80) and understands the multiplicity of paths in exploring nature as an inevitable consequence of the variety of human experiences and perspectives: "Vielmehr will er, daß wir den eignen Weg verfolgen, weil jeder neue Weg durch neue Länder geht, und jeder endlich zu diesen Wohnungen, zu dieser heiligen Heimath wieder führet (I: 82). Today we may lack the certainty that we are in fact going "Immer nach Hause" (I: 325) or else choose, as does Alice Kuzniar, to place the stress on "Immer" rather than "nach Hause".[20] But Novalis can still serve as a welcome companion as we search for a realization of the ecological insight that the earth is indeed our οἶκος, is indeed our home, and it remains for us to continue the writing of texts that Novalis left unended in more ways than one.

---

[19] Cf. John Neubauer, "Nature as Construct" in: *Literature and Science as Modes of Expression*, ed. Frederick Amrine, (Dordrecht, Boston, London: Kluwer, 1989), p. 129–140; esp. p. 135–137.

[20] Alice Kuzniar, *Delayed Endings, Nonclosure in Novalis and Hölderlin*, (Athens: U of Georgia P, 1987), p. 83.

Arnd Bohm

The Desublimated Body: Gottfried August Bürger

IF ONE WERE TEMPTED to sum up the most profound development in the study of eighteenth-century texts of the last twenty years, a possible response would be "the return of the body." From various disciplines and for diverse reasons, there is a new awareness of the fact that human existence begins with embodiment and that relations — personal, family, social, economic or political — begin with our individual physical being.[1] The importance attached to such apparently simple insights would have baffled observers from earlier eras, as it puzzled non-European cultures. Why all the fuss? The answer resides in the complex intertwining of the history of the rise of the middle class in Europe with a puritanizing campaign aimed at covering, disciplining and defining the body.

Nowhere was the triumph of the mind ("Geist") more secure than in the German territories of the eighteenth century, where the middle class was able to assert itself in both directions, against rulers and against the peasants. A basic contradiction between freedom and license resulted from the fact that by enforcing disciplines of the body upon rulers, the bourgeoisie was able to gain a measure of autonomy. As for the peasantry, they were subjected to increasing control of their bodies — exemplified in the tragic history of the treatment of unwed mothers[2]

---

[1] Nothing approximating a complete list of relevant works is possible. Major points of triangulation are provided by Michel Foucault, *Discipline and Punish: The Birth of the Prison*, trans. Alan Sheridan (New York: Vintage, 1979); Dorinda Outram, *The Body and the French Revolution: Sex, Class and Political Culture* (New Haven and London: Yale UP); Elaine Scarry, *The Body in Pain: The Making and Unmaking of the World* (New York and Oxford: Oxford University Press, 1985); and John O'Neill, *Five Bodies: The Human Shape of Modern Society* (Ithaca and London: Cornell UP, 1985).

[2] On unwed mothers and infanticide as a theme in German literature of the time, see Hamilton Beck, "Of Two Minds About the Death Penalty: Hippel's Account of a Case of Infanticide," *Studies in Eighteenth-Century Culture* 18 (1988): 123-140; and Helga Stipa Madland, "Infanticide as Fiction: Goethe's *Urfaust* and Schiller's 'Kindsmörderin' as Models," *The German Quarterly* 62.1 (1989): 27-38. For a socio-historical perspective, see David Sabean,"Unehelichkeit: Ein Aspekt sozialer Reproduktion kleinbäuerlicher Produzenten: Zu einer Analyse dörflicher Quellen um 1800," in *Klassen und Kultur: Sozialanthropologische Perspektiven in der Geschichtsschreibung*, ed. Robert M. Berdahl, et. al. (Frankfurt a. M.: Syndikat, 1982): 54-76. An overview of the theory

— under the rubric of "improvement." The intellectual components of the bourgeois program were the elaboration of extreme philosophical idealism and, in the sphere of literature, the ideal of a "classical" norm for embodied behavior.[3] The paradigm of German literary classicism was Goethe's drama *Iphigenie auf Tauris* (1799-80), where the repression of private feelings and physical desires is exalted: good deeds are to result from self-denial and a harmonious society will be composed of disembodied souls.[4]

There was another side to Goethe, of course.[5] But the alliance of idealistic philosophy and the norms of the *Klassik* have made it especially difficult to recover any body-related themes for German lierary history of the eighteenth century.[6] Without Swift, Fielding, Rousseau or de Sade, obvious gateways where-

---

of practical Enlightenment by the state is provided in Marc Raeff's *The Well-Ordered Police State: Social and Institutional Change through Law in the Germanies and Russia, 1600-1800* (New Haven and London: Yale UP, 1983): 43-179.

[3] On the background to the German concept of "Klassik," see Reinhold Grimm and Jost Hermand, eds., *Die Klassik-Legende* (Frankfurt a. M.: Athenäum, 1971), and in particular Max L.Baeumer's essay "Der Begriff 'klassisch' bei Goethe und Schiller," 17-49. Although a central text for the Klassik was Winckelmann's *Gedanken über die Nachahmung der griechischen Werke in der Malerei und Bildhauerkunst* (1756), little mention was made of his insistence upon the priority of the body — and the nude body — for the Greek ideal of beauty.

[4] Thus, Kenneth D. Weisinger, *The Classical Façade: A Nonclassical Reading of Goethe's Classicism* (University Park and London: The Pennsylvania State UP, 1988), p. 102, continues to ask "Can in fact the ethical be grounded in the purely human?" And Ursula Segebrecht, "Götter, Helden und Goethe: Zur Geschichtsdeutung in Goethes *Iphigenie auf Tauris*," in *Klassik und Moderne: Die Weimarer Klassik als historisches Ereignis und Herausforderung im kulturgeschichtlichen Prozeß*, ed. Karl Richter and Jörg Schönert (Stuttgart: J. B. Metzler, 1983): 175-193, comes to the position "Zum Handeln herausgefordert, zeigt Iphigenie ihr neues Menschsein zu allererst darin, daß sie dort, wo es um den Menschen geht und sein Recht zu leben, gesellschaftliche Bedingungen, gesellschaftliche Rollenzwänge nicht zu übernehmen bereit ist, sondern aus ihnen heraustritt und ihnen gegenüber die *Freiheit der Person* behauptet" (185). It is an odd notion that one can be "purely human" or a "free person" without a body.

[5] See for example Chapter 3, "Satanskult: *Walpurgisnacht*," in Albrecht Schöne, *Götterzeichen-Liebeszauber-Satanskult: Neuer Einblick in alte Goethetexte* (München: C. H. Beck, 1982): 107-230.

[6] The German discussion, in connection primarily with the 18th century, may be charted via Erika Fischer-Lichte, "Theatre and the Civilizing Process: An Approach to the History of Acting," in *Interpreting the Theatrical Past: Essays in the Historiography of Performance*, ed. Thomas Postlewait and Bruce A. McConachie (Iowa City: U of Iowa P, 1989): 19-36; Hans Ulrich Gumbrecht, "'Mens Sana' und 'Körperloses Spiel'/ 'Sinnloses Treten' und 'In Corpore Sano'," *Sprache im technischen Zeitalter* 92 (December 1984): 262-278; Utz Jaeggle, "Im Schatten des Körpers: Vorüberlegungen zu einer Volkskunde der Körperlichkeit," *Zeitschrift für Volkskunde* 76.2 (1980): 169-188; Wolfgang Kemp, "Die Beredsamkeit des Leibes: Körpersprache als künstlerisches und gesellschaftliches Problem der bürgerlichen Emanzipation," *Städel-Jahrbuch* NF 5 (1975): 111-134; Gert Mattenklott, "Körperpolitik oder das Schwinden der Sinne," in *"Postmoderne" oder Der Kampf um die Zukunft: Die Kontroverse in Wissenschaft, Kunst und Gesellschaft*, ed. Peter Kemper

by the body might be recovered for discourse, German literary history continues to occlude the body.[7] Against this background, it is necessary to re-assess the negative reception granted a writer like Gottfried August Bürger, for his open reliance upon sensuality, his frequent public allusions to the wants and symptoms of the body, and his carnevalization of the body in texts remain an embarrassment to the established view of German literature. More than that, Bürger's reminders that politics originates in the body place him within a radical tradition near the German Jacobins and later writers such as Georg Büchner and Bertolt Brecht.

Bürger (1747-1794) is marginalized in being remembered, if at all, either as the author of the popular ballad "Leonore"[8] or as the object of a devastating review of his works by Friedrich Schiller in 1789. Unlike J.M.R. Lenz or Büchner, whose sad personal lives have achieved a certain legendary status, and with whom Bürger had much in common, his career is hardly known. His pathetic death in 1794 at the age of 47, pleading with the University of Göttingen for some small financial assistance to stave off hunger, ended a life which should be better known as an example of the harsh reality of literary professions in the eighteenth century.[9] The surface reasons for Bürger's obscurity are not hard to find. First, there were the negative pronouncements upon him made not only by Schiller, but also by Goethe, typically the kiss of death in German letters. Goethe coldly described Bürger's ultimate failure as true to type: "Es ist traurig anzusehen, wie ein außerordentlicher Mensch sich gar oft mit sich selbst, seinen Umständen, seiner Zeit herumwürgt, ohne auf einen Zweig zu kommen: Trauriges Beispiel Bürger."[10]

(Frankfurt a. M.: Fischer Taschenbuch, 1988): 231-252; and Liliane Weissberg, "Language's Wound: Herder, Philoctetes and the Origin of Speech," *Modern Language Notes* 104.3 (1989): 548-579.

[7] A major attack on the absence of the body in idealist German philosophy has been made by Peter Sloterdijk, *Kritik der zynischen Vernunft* (Frankfurt a. M.: Suhrkamp, 1983).

[8] See the reclamation of Bürger for the canon by Gert Ueding, "Von der unheilbaren Liebe als Stimulans der Poesie: Der Dichter Gottfried August Bürger," in his *Die anderen Klassiker: Literarische Porträts aus zwei Jahrhunderten* (München: C.H. Beck, 1986): 13-34; and Lore Kaim-Kloock, *Gottfried August Bürger: Zum Problem der Volkstümlichkeit in der Lyrik* (Berlin: Rütten & Loening, 1963): 170-205. "Lenore" also had a considerable reception in England, as documented by Evelyn B. Jolles, *G.A. Bürgers Ballade "Lenore" in England* (Regensburg: Verlag Hans Carl, 1974).

[9] On Bürger's life, see Günter Häntzschel, *Gottfried August Bürger* (München: C. H. Beck, 1988); Gerhard Kluge, "Gottfried August Bürger," in *Deutsche Dichter des 18. Jahrhunderts: Ihr Leben und Werk*, ed. Benno von Wiese (Berlin: Erich Schmicdt, 1977): 594-618; and Wm. A. Little, *Gottfried August Bürger* (New York: Twayne, 1974).

[10] Johann Wolfgang von Goethe, *Werke: Hamburger Ausgabe in 14 Bänden*, ed. Erich Trunz, Vol. 12: *Schriften zur Kunst*, ed. Erich Trunz with Herbert von Einem (München: DTV, 1982): 531.

Then there has been the problem of the lack of a comprehensive edition of Bürger's works.[11] Finally, it is only recently that it has become theoretically possible to cope with Bürger's work, for his was a voice from below, and German literary historians have not been keen to hear from the underground.

Ironically, Bürger had very much wanted to be known as a spokesman for the people. It was in relation to the "Volk" that he had introduced himself in the 1789 collection of his poems:

> In dem Sinne, wie ich ein Volksdichter, oder lieber ein populärer Dichter zu sein wünsche, ist Homer, wegen der spiegelhellen Durchsichtigkeit und Temperatur seines Gesangstromes, der größte Volksdichter aller Völker und Zeiten, sind es, mehr oder weniger, alle großen Dichter, auch die unsrigen, und gerade in ihren allgemein geliebtesten und unsterblichen Versen, unendlich mehr als ich gewesen.[12] (C I: 8-9)

By positing himself as a "popular poet," Bürger helped to provoke the negative response from Schiller which disputed the validity of Bürger's claim to the title. According to Schiller, Bürger could not be a genuine poet of the people because his work remained too bound to its personal and idiosyncratic origins. What Schiller required was rather an abstracted attitude:

> Als der aufgeklärte, verfeinerte *Wortführer der Volksgefühle* würde er dem hervorströmenden, Sprache suchenden Affekt der Liebe, der Freude, der Andacht, der Traurigkeit, der Hoffnung u.a.m. einen reinem und geistreichem Text unterlegen; er würde, indem er ihnen den Ausdruck lieh, sich zum Herrn dieser Affekte machen und ihren rohen, gestaltlosen, oft tierischen Ausbruch noch auf den Lippen des Volks veredeln.[13]

The genealogy of Schiller's ideas derived as much from his medical training as from aesthetic theory.[14] Neither had any place for bodies which were not perfect and exemplary. Therapeutics and aesthetics combined in Schiller's proposition that the poet's task should be, and Bürger's should have been, to produce "entire beings" in literature:

---

[11] The gap was only partially filled with the appearance of the *Sämtliche Werke* (München: Hanser, 1987), edited by Günter and Hiltrud Häntzschel.

[12] Johann Gottfried Bürger, *Bürgers Gedichte in zwei Teilen*, ed. Ernst Consentius (Berlin and Leizpig: Deutsches Verlagshaus Bong & Co., [1914]): 1: 8-9. References to this edition will be made parenthetically as *Gedichte*, with volume and page numbers.

[13] Friedrich Schiller, "Über Bürgers Gedichte," in F. Schiller, *Werke in drei Bänden*, ed. Herbert G. Göpfert with Gerhard Fricke (München: Hanser, 1981): II: 627-638, here p. 630.

[14] See John Neubauer, "The Freedom of the Machine: On Mechanism, Materialism, and the Young Schiller," *Eighteenth-Century Studies* 15.1 (1981): 275-290; and Walter Hinderer, "Utopische Elemente in Schiller's ästhetischer Anthropologie," in *Literarische Utopie-Entwürfe*, ed. Hiltrud Gnüg (Frankfurt a. M.: Suhrkamp, 1982): 173-186.

> Bei der Vereinzelung und getrennten Wirksamkeit unsrer Geisteskräfte, die der erweiterte Kreis des Wissens und die Absonderung der Berufsgeschäfte notwendig macht, ist es die Dichtkunst beinahe allein, welche die getrennten Kräfte der Seele wieder in Vereinigung bringt, welche Kopf und Herz, Scharfsinn und Witz, Vernunft und Einbildungskraft in harmonischem Bunde beschäftigt, welche gleichsam den *ganzen Menschen* in uns wieder herstellt.[15]

Schiller sees the problems of the "whole person" in terms of the mind which has been fragmented by specialized knowledge and must be reunified. In the process, actual lived experience would become irrelevant.[16] All sensations are to be subordinated to the abstract mind, if necessary by sheer willpower. The body is doubly displaced in Schiller's program, for even where sensations can be integrated into the text, they must be those of an idealized presence — a pure vessel filled with laudable sentiments. Given such premises, it followed that Schiller should also have objected to what he considered Bürger's illegitimate intermingling of popular elements into the text: "Hr. B *vermischt* sich nicht selten mit dem Volk, zu dem er sich herablassen sollte, und anstatt es scherzend und spielend zu sich hinaufzuziehen, gefällt es ihm oft, sich ihm gleich zu machen."[17] For the idealist Schiller, Bürger's error was to identify with the people as they lived, when he should have set his work above experience, in order to offer as a utopian goal the idealized community of a timeless German readership. The larger context for Schiller's criticism was his adherence to and advocacy of the aesthetics of the sublime, with which he strove to defend the autonomy of art and poetry. What Schiller could perceive but not tolerate was the contrary aesthetic upon which Bürger had developed.[18]

Bürger admittedly had not helped his case through the introduction to his collection, which was intended as something of an advertisement. He was quite aware of the influence of criticism and of the supremacy of the ideals of the Weimar Classicists. He was also well-versed in dissembling, after years of trying

---

[15] Schiller, "Über Bürgers Gedichte," II: 627.

[16] "Nur die heitre, die ruhige Seele gebiert das Vollkommene. Kampf mit äußern Lagen und Hypochondrie, welche überhaupt jede Geisteskraft lähmen, dürfen am allerwenigsten das Gemüt des Dichters belasten, der sich von der Gegenwart loswickeln und frei und kühn in die Welt der Ideale emporschweben soll. Wenn es auch noch so sehr in seinem Busen stürmt, so müsse Sonnenklarheit seine Stirne umfließen." Schiller, "Über Bürgers Gedichte," 2: 638.

[17] Schiller, "Über Bürgers Gedichte," 2: 631.

[18] Because the basic assumption is that Schiller must have been correct in his *interpretation* of Bürger, commentaries on the controversy tend to side with Schiller. See for example Walter Hinderer, "Schiller und Bürger: Die ästhetische Kontroverse als Paradigma," *Jahrbuch des Freien Deutschen Hochstifts* (1986): 130-154; and Helmut Koopmann, "Der Dichter als Kunstrichter: Zu Schillers Rezensionsstrategie," *Jahrbuch der Deutschen Schillergesellschaft* 20 (1976): 229-246, here pp. 243-244. Rather more open to Bürger's position is Jürgen Bolten, *Friedrich Schiller: Poesie, Reflexion und gesellschaftliche Selbstdeutung* (München: Fink, 1985): 195-201.

to adapt to the public demands of bourgeois conventionality. Nothing could be more typical of this dissembling than the "confession" in which Bürger stated that he was speaking too much about himself: "Es thut mir leid, daß ich hier so viel von mir selbst reden muß, welches, wie ich wohl weiß, nicht fein läßt. Ich bin mir indessen bewußt, daß ich von mir selbst so unbefangen und gleichgültig, als von einem fremden Manne rede" (*Gedichte* 1: 9). Yes, Bürger was speaking of himself "as if he were speaking of a stranger," precisely because in the effort to establish his public persona, he could not reveal much about Bürger the person. Schiller was quick to pick on the difference between the role and the person, and to notice that while the introduction invoked a poetry dedicated to the cause of the sublime, the poems undermined the pretense. Bürger's aesthetic was not based upon the sublime but upon an aesthetics localized in the lived body, whence it might manifest itself as the beautiful, the ordinary, the grotesque or even the ugly. Furthermore, the bodies which now appeared in the texts were those of the "Volk" as common people, those who were neither aristocrats nor members of the middle classes, but lived at the bottom and margins of eighteenth-century society. In the extended discussion of the contribution which Bürger made to German literature by re-invigorating the ballad as a genre, this dimension has generally been overlooked. Yet it is important. Bürger's insertion of the embodied experience of marginalized members of society represented a politics and poetics of transgression. In Bürger it is possible to observe the dissolution of the bond between the subjected bourgeois body and literary textualization.[19]

The three elements which repeatedly returned Bürger to the lived body as the locus of production, both of texts and of history, were poverty, sickness, and sexuality. There can be no doubt that a man who until his death was continually struggling to make ends meet, to be able to buy food and keep a roof over his head, was aware of corporeal existence most directly. The body could not be kept at a distance by theorizing or idealizing under such dire conditions. Illness, exacerbated by poor diet and overwork, was also a constant in Bürger's life, as his letters frequently testify. For example, he wrote to his publisher Dieterich on March 5, 1781:

> Stelle dir den Jammer vor! Alle von 1ten Januar 1748 an begangene Sünden meines Madensacks brachen in einem ganz infamen Geschwür gerade über der Pulsader meiner rechten Hand hervor. In kurzem waren meine Hand und Arm so dick, wie mein Lende, und ich konte die Hand nicht so viel rühren, um nur einen

---

[19] Michel de Certeau, *The Practice of Everyday Life*, trans. Steven F. Rendall (Berkeley, Los Angeles and London: U of California P, 1984): 131-153; Frances Barker, *The Tremulous Private Body: Essays on Subjection* (London and New York: Methuen, 1984); and Hans Ulrich Gumbrecht, "Beginn von 'Literatur'/ Abschied vom Körper?" in *Der Ursprung von Literatur: Medien, Rollen, Kommunikationssituationen zwischen 1450 und 1650*, ed. Gisela Smolka-Koerdt, Peter M. Spangenberg, and Dagmar Tillmann-Bartylla (München: Fink, 1988): 15-50 map the intersection of bodies and texts in an exemplary fashion.

Buchstaben zu machen. Vorige Woche war die ärgste Marter Woche meines Lebens, das Geschwür ist endlich aufgegangen und bald wird der Schade wieder heil seyn.[20]

From a psychoanalytic/psychosomatic perspective, the imagery with which Bürger describes his illness and the recovery is revealing. Like a fleshly text, one limb has swollen with the memory of the sins of the entire body, thereby blocking any writing, any confessional re-textualization. The opening of the boil in turn enables him to write again, so that the body publishes, as it were, its agonized history. Numerous equally graphic passages about the state of the physical body could be quoted from the letters, indicating Bürger's ongoing concern with his physical being. What is striking is Bürger's continued effort to give voice to the body, including genital and scatological aspects, in written texts. The semi-public forum of the letters allowed more freedom than the published literary works, yet Bürger also made some extraordinary efforts at the integration of body and text.

In the poetry intended for publication, Bürger could hardly express the pains and needs of the body explicitly or directly. The body's actual history could in most cases only be made public through allegories and discrete allusions. In the process of textualizing what the body knew, Bürger often could not speak in the first person, for the market constituted by eighteenth-century middle-class readers would not have paid for the reports of the life of a nobody. Just tolerable for the conventionalized taste was a poem such as "Zum Spatz," which picked up on the topos of the caged bird as metonym for the constrained poet. Worth noting in this text are the contorted stance of the speaker and the intensity of the inscribed violence. How power moves with social roles is indicated by the shifting voices. Until the final two lines, it is difficult to decide whether the speaker is foe or friend:

> Ich sein Despot und Er mein Sklav'!
> Bei seinem Spatzvolk!

Later, the speaker shifts positions:

> Doch, daß ich stets eingedenk Ihm sei,
> Die Freiheit sei ein güldner Schatz,
> So hudelt man Ihn erst, Herr Spatz,
> Und scheucht Ihn hin und her, husch! husch!
> Nun Fenster auf! Hinaus zu Busch! (*Gedichte* 1: 225)

Are humanity or servility responsible for the bird's freedom? Given that the bird represents the situation of a writer, when the speaker is also a writer, matters become complicated. The poem does not remain on the level of idealized relation-

---

[20] Gottfried August Bürger, *Mein Scharmantes Geldmännchen: Gottfried August Bürgers Briefwechsel mit seinem Verleger Dieterich*, ed. Ulrich Joost (Göttingen: Wallstein-Verlag, 1988): 78.

ships, but instead foregrounds the implications of arbitrary despotism for the writer as a human being. The verbalized threat depicts the violence that might be done to the body of the bird, or the speaker-writer:

> Hör er nun,
> Was all mit ihm ich könnte thun.
> Ihn zupfen, rupfen, halsumdrehn —
> Da wird nicht Hund noch Hahn nach krähn,
> Zerschlagen ihn mit einem Hieb,
> Und das mit Recht, Er Galgendieb. (*Gedichte* 1: 225)

These images have been projected by the body as its anxiety about the government which reigns by using force, torture, and the threat of force. We recognize in the cavalier mistreatment of the helpless bird the disciplining of the body meted out by eighteenth-century rulers against writers, such as Schubart, who did not strike the proper note.[21] Bürger dare not say, perhaps could not bring to the level of words, that he felt the rule of society and law working him over thusly.

Not only formal political institutions operated as constraints upon the body and upon texts. Comportment of the body was also regulated by the imposition of courtly style upon posture. The allegorical poem "Mamselle La Regle" identifies the regulation of the literary text with a social discipline of the body. The personified "rule of style" links the postures of the text and of the body. Both are subject to the control of convention:

> 'Fein gerade!
> Hübsch Füßchen aus, und einwärts hübsch die Wade!
> Den Rücken schlank! Fein Hals und Kopf empor!
> Zurück die Schulter! Bauch ein! Brust hervor! (*Gedichte* 1: 226)

The German-speaking reader will hear in these instructions overtones of the military as well as of the schools, for both were also institutions by which the absolutist state inscribed correct mental and physical attitudes upon subjects.[22] A parallel passage, displaying the similar conjunction of forces actually at work, is found in Act I, Scene 4 of Lenz's *Der Hofmeister* (1774), where the Major is beating posture into his son:

---

[21] Duke Carl Eugen of Württemberg had Christian Friedrich Daniel Schubart (1739-1791) arrested in 1777 because of his political writings. After 377 days of solitary confinement, Schubart remained in prison without trial until 1778.

[22] For an introduction to this complex topic, see Georges Vigarello, "The Upward Training of the Body from the Age of Chivalry to Courtly Chivalry," in *Fragments for a History of the Human Body*, ed. Michel Feher with Ramona Naddaff and Nadia Tazi (New York: Zone, 1989): 2: 149-196; Bernd Jürgen Warncken, "Bürgerliche Emanzipation und aufrechter Gang: Zur Geschichte eines Haltungsideals," *Das Argument* 179 (1990): 39-52; and Henning Eichberg, "Geometrie als barocke Verhaltensnorm: Fortifikation und Exerzitien," *Zeitschrift für historische Forschung* 4 (1977): 17-50. Eichberg observes the political implications of the "undisciplined" bodies and irregular military formations of the American and French revolutionary armies (p. 40).

> Lippel! ich bitt Dich um tausend Gottes willen, den Kopf grad. Den Kopf in die Höhe, Junge! *richtet ihn* Tausend Sakkerment den Kopf aus den Schultern! oder ich zerbrech Dir Dein Rückenbein in tausendmillionen Stücken .... Ich will dich zu Tode hauen — *giebt ihm eine Ohrfeige* Schon wieder wie ein Fragezeichen? Er läßt sich nicht sagen.[23]

The Major reads the son's slouch as a text of disobedience: therefore the body must be corrected according to the edicts of authority.

Although an interaction between texts and bodies was possible, there could be no dialogue between the government and the subject about the latter's position. Instructions about whether to speak or be silent, whether to stand straight or kneel came in one direction, from above. Only in the guise of fiction could the subject respond, challenging authority by reminding its spokesmen of their own embodiedness, their carnality and mortality. Bürger's poem "Frau Schnips" is a witty example of the reversal. The dead woman responds at the entrance to heaven to charges that her sins of the flesh should preclude her being admitted. Citing the Bible in rebuttal, she points out that every kind of sin has already been recorded in Scriptutre. Although they might now be angelic, the denizens of heaven were once beings in human bodies. The consequences of embodiedness begin with Adam:

> Ei, zupfte sich Herr Erdenkloß
> Doch nur an eigner Nase!
> Denn was man ist, das ist man bloß
> Von seinem Apfelfraße.
>
> So gut wie Er, denk' ich zur Ruh
> Noch Platz hier zu gewinnen. (*Gedichte* 1: 182)

The label "clod of earth" is less rude than it is etymologically correct, for Adam's name refers back to his creation from the dust and underscores his material existence. Since the Fall, no one has been able to avoid being born on earth or managed to evade the body. The poem dismantles the illusion of transcendental existence. One after another, biblical figures are confronted with the argument that while she may be no better than those who have already been saved, Frau Schnips has been no worse. Even a king such as Solomon will have had something to confess:

> Sieb'n hunder Weiber auf der Streu,
> Und extra noch darneben
> Drei hundert — — Andre! Meiner Treu!
> Das war ein züchtig Leben! (*Gedichte* 1: 184)

---

[23] Jacob Michael Reinhold Lenz, *Gesammelte Werke in vier Bänden*, ed. Richard Daunicht (München: Fink, 1967): 1: 46.

Of course, she wins in the end. Despite its allegorical framework and the fact that Bürger had in the main taken the story from the English ballad "The wanton wife of Bath," he had great difficulty in getting it published because of the threat of censorship. Goeckingk, the editor of the *Musenalmanach*, found it unsuitable for polite mixed company.[24] Beyond the taint of blasphemy, the poem offended against the social order which regulated matters of sex and sensuality. Even Bürger's appended apology, in which he reminded readers that the messages were already in the Bible, did not mollify readers such as Goethe or Schiller.

Two other short texts manifest a similar projection from the body through the imagination against those in power. "Der Bauer an seinen Fürsten," one of the most astounding political poems in German from the eighteenth century, develops its arguments on the basis of the body's rebellion.[25] As in "Frau Schnips," the rhetorical strategy is to remind those in power that on the plane of emobdiment they are no better than other human beings:

Wer bist du, Fürst, daß über mich
Herrollen frei dein Wagenrad,
Dein Roß mich stampfen darf?

Wer bist du Fürst, daß in mein Fleisch
Dein Freund, dein Jagdhund, ungebläut
Darf Klau- und Rachen haun?

Wer bist du? daß durch Saat und Forst
Das Hurra deiner Jagd mich treibt,
Entatmet wie das Wild?

Die Saat, so deine Jagd zertritt,
Was Roß und Hund und du verschlingst,
Das Brot, du Fürst, ist mein!

Du Fürst hast nie bei Egg' und Pflug,
Hast nie den Erntegang durchschwitzt!
Mein, mein ist Fleiß und Brot! —

Ha! du wärst Obrigkeit von Gott?
Gott spendet Segen aus! du raubst!
Du nicht von Gott! Tyrann! (*Gedichte* 1: 55-56)

The poem is a more acute version of "Frau Schnips." Now the speaker is alive and the opponent is a ruler in the political realm of eighteenth-century Europe.

---

[24] "Frau Schnips ist schlechterdings keine Gesellschaft für die Herren und Dämchen welche den Almanach lesen ... . Ohn alles Bedenken aber laßt es in das Museum einrücken, denn dieses wird doch mehrenteils nur von Männern gelesen." *Gedichte* 2: 310.

[25] Häntzschel, *Gottfried August Bürger*: 70-73; Little, *Gottfried August Bürger*: 72.

The strategy of the argument again draws upon Scripture by reminding the nobleman that everyone was born to labor after the Fall, earning bread with the body's sweat. The despotic state, where many work and a few play, is seen as a violation of the divine economy. Not idealized principles of liberty or the desire to participate in a heroic scripted history lead to revolt; only the "too much!" of an exhausted, tortured body leads to this articulation of self-awareness.[26] What is striking is the fact that the peasant here gives voice to his own feelings, disrupting the social illusion that only the upper classes could have emotions worth knowing. Bürger has assigned to the peasant the role of advocate for embodied passions and interests.[27] The laboring body has become aware of its subjectivity and is now able to articulate the sentiments which are grounded in physical experience. Again, the stance of the speaker is worth noting: a peasant known only through the title speaks, in fictional direct speech, to the Prince, without using the shielding honorific "Sie." The "Du" is not the companionable "Du" of a Goethe adressing Duke Karl August as social or intellectual equal, but is an accusatory definition of the Other whose presence excludes and yet establishes the Self. The renaming of the Prince as Tyrant is the moment when the speaking Self translates the body's knowledge of hunger, weariness and fear into the language of the body politic.

The short prose text "Der Maulwurf und der Gärtner" is a remarkable political fable. The conflict is between a mole, who has been digging up the flowers, and an infuriated gardener, who threatens to kill the animal. The mole is an archetypal representative of "those who are below."[28] In this instance, the harmless creature tries to defend itself by pointing to its usefulness in the economic sphere:

'Gnade!' flehte der Maulwurf, 'da ich dir doch sonst nicht unnütz bin. Ich vertilge die Regenmaden und manches Ungeziefer, das seine Pflanzungen verwüstet.' (*Gedichte* 1: 240)

The gardener refuses to listen and replies with brute force:

'Hole dich der Henker,' versetzte der Gärtner, 'wenn du Tugend mit Untugend aufwiegst!' und schlug ihn ohne weitern Prozeß tot. (*Gedichte* 1:240)

---

[26] For the background to this process, see Oskar Negt and Alexander Kluge, *Geschichte und Eigensinn: Geschichtliche Organisation der Arbeitsvermögen* (Frankfurt a. M.: Zweitausendeins, 1981).

[27] On the passions and the interests, see Albert O. Hirschman, *The Passions and the Interests: Political Arguments for Capitalism before Its Triumph* (Princeton: Princeton UP, 1977); and Winfried Schulze, "Vom Gemeinnutz zum Eigennutz: Über den Normenwandel in der ständischen Gesellschaft der frühen Neuzeit," *Historische Zeitschrift* 243.3 (1986): 591-626.

[28] Karlheinz Stierle, "Der Maulwurf im Bildfeld," in *Bewegung und Stillstand in Metaphern und Mythen: Fallstudien zum Verhältnis von elementarem Wissen und Literatur im 19. Jahrhundert*, ed. Jürgen Link and Wulf Wülfing (Stuttgart: Klett-Cotta, 1984): 121-141.

So much, then for the possibility of a discourse of reason between those from below and those who wield power and control the economic order. The mole, whose mere effort to stay alive has distrubed the calm surface of things, is dispatched without further ado. Like the caged sparrow or the peasant, the mole represents what could happen in the eighteenth century to those who refused to let themselves be blended into the background as part of "the natural order." By speaking, by giving voice to their sufferings, these beings insisted upon the difference between bodies with consciousness and mute objects.

Given that the fable of the mole represented accurately the realities of the distribution of power in eighteenth-century German society, the question that remains is why Bürger failed to conform. Why did he not keep silent? Goethe was correct in his cynical diagnosis of Bürger's lapses when he wrote to him suggesting that Bürger was inherently disposed to dissatisfaction with bourgeois society:

> Die Unzufriedenheit mit Ihrem Zustande, die Sie mir zu erkennen geben, scheint mir so sehr aus dem Verhältnis Ihres Innersten, Ihrer Talente, Begriffe und Wünsche, zu dem Zustande unserer bürgerlichen Verfassung, zu liegen, daß ich nicht glaube, es werde Sie die Veränderung des Ortes, außer einem geringen Mehr oder Weniger, jemals befriedigen können ... . Tüchtige Kinder dieser eingeschränkten Erde, denen im Schweiß ihres Angesichts ihr Brot schmecken kann, sind allein gebaut, sich darin leidlich zu befinden, und nach ihren Fähigkeit und Tugenden das Gute und Ordentliche zu wirken.[29]

The reference to the Biblical injunction (Genesis 4.19) is cited rather cruelly by Goethe, reminding Bürger that he had better be contented with the human condition of hunger and labor. Yet Bürger refused, and this has puzzled his biographers.

If good behavior and polite silence had simply been a question of acceding to external social pressure, then perhaps Bürger might have been able to conform. However, the roots of his resistance were inextricably bound up with the sexual dimension of physical being. The texts in which Bürger deliberately spoke of topics such as male and female anatomy, intercourse or sexual desire have earned him enduring opprobrium. Little is gained by labelling such elements of Bürger's work "pornographic" or "obscene." They were evidently intended by him as subversions of the controls imposed by genre and censorship that excluded physical being from textualization. In one of the few articles dealing with Bürger from this perspective, Alfons Höger has shown how Bürger subverted the traditions of the "Anacreontic" love-lyric, which had been imitated from the French courtly tradition, by inserting a body-based sensuality into chaste texts.[30]

---

[29] Johann Wolfgang von Goethe, *Werke*, Sophien-Ausgabe, Part 4: *Briefe*, Vol. 5: *Weimar, 7. November 1780-30. Juni 1782*) (Weimar: Böhlau, 1889), letter of February 2, 1782. The letter was on a par with Schiller's review in devastating Bürger's self-confidence.

[30] Alfons Höger, "'Und etwas anders noch ...': Galanterie und Sinnlichkeit in den Gedichten G.A. Bürgers," *Text und Kontext* 9.2 (1981): 250-270.

In many of his published love lyrics, Bürger veered towards an explicit physical dimension. In "Stutzertändelei," the exchange between Cupid and the woman leads towards a suggestive conclusion. Cupid is to transform himself into a fly and explore the hidden recesses of the female body:

> In eine kleine Fliege —
> Siehst du, was ich erfand! —
> Verwandle dich und fliege
> Auf ihrer Schnürbrust Rand.
>
> Dort gleite durch die Falte,
> Im zarten Musselin,
> Bis zu dem tiefen Spalte
> Des warmen Busens hin. (*Gedichte* 1: 28)

Slightly more risqué was "Collin und Juliette," in which the prohibition against speaking openly about sexual matters becomes the point of the wit. The teasing refrain "Ich mag es nicht zu sagen,/ Und etwas andres noch" (*Gedichte* 2: 163) gains increasingly explicit values as it mocks the pretenses of bowdlerized pastoral poetry:

> Des Schäfers banges Sehnen
> Ist nun gestillt — es floß
> Ein Strom von Freuenthränen
> In der Geliebten Schoß
> Und etwas andres noch, —
> Ich wag es nicht zu sagen, —
> Und etwas andres noch; —
> Wer wird nach allem fragen?

This went too far; the poem was not published in Germany until 1905. However, Bürger wrote other poems which transgressed even more against the norms of his readers, for they spoke openly about male anatomy and desires. One such poem was written as a parallel to "Das Mädel, das ich meine," which had described the ideal of womanhood in the conventions of polite, sublimated discourse. No reader then could have taken offense at the rarefied description of the perfect woman, done in a series of stereotypical images:

> Wer hat das Rot auf Weiß gemalt,
> Das von des Mädels Wange strahlt? —
> Der liebe Gott! der hat's gethan,
> Der Pfirsichblüte malen kann;
> Der hat das Rot auf weiß gemalt,
> Das von des Mädels Wange strahlt. (*Gedichte* 1: 65)

Bürger had also produced a similar poem about the ideal, entitled fittingly enough "Männerkeuschheit." There he had described being a man in sublime language far removed from any actual body:

Sein Auge funkelt dunkelhell,
Wie ein krystallner Schattenquell.
Sein Antlitz strahlt, wie Morgenrot;
Auf Nas' und Stirn herrscht Machtgebot.

Das Machtgebot, das d'rauf regiert,
Wird hui! durch seinen Arm vollführt.
Denn der schnellt aus, wie Federstahl;
Sein Schwerthieb ist ein Wetterstrahl. (*Gedichte* 1: 75)

Given Bürger's own anxieties about his physique and about his continuing struggle against illness, it is hard to take this poem as more than a series of clichés. This was the normative language in which the body could be discussed in public.

In very different texts, Bürger mocked the polite discourse of ideal bodies. One was a parodistic parallel to "Das Mädchen, das ich meine" and proceeded to enumerate parts of the male anatomy in gross detail:

Wer hat die Arsback ausgestopft,
Die sich so prall' anfühlt und klopft? —
Der große Satler hats gethan,
Der Pferdelenden polstern kan;
Der hat die Arsback ausgestopft,
Die sich so prall' anfühlt und klopft. (*Gedichte* 2: 248)

Editors who might hope to ban the text from Bürger's works are hindered by the fact that he sent a copy to Dieterich, so that the authorship is clear.[31] Whether he also wrote "An die Feinde des Priaps" is more circumstantial, but nonetheless convincing. Apparently it was his contribution to a small competition with Johann Heinrich Voß, who provided "An Priap" and Friedrich Leopold Graf zu Stolberg, who offered "Wahl meiner künftigen Gattin und ihre Eigenschaften." All three texts are patently obscene in the sense that they challenge the normative aesthetic of the period. Bürger's ode to the penis is a ribald exercise in saying the unspeakable. The disembodied figures of classical mythology are satirically shown draped in bodies whose grotesqueness undermines their function in the German Klassik:

Charon, beim Überfahren,
Fuchst alles rauch von Haaren,
Schont auch die Votzen nicht;
Pluto fuchst Proserpinen,
Und Luchse fuchst Luchsinnen,
Warum denn Menschen nicht?[32]

---

[31] Bürger, *Mein Scharmantes Geldmännchen*, p. 73, letter of July 20, 1780.

[32] *Dein Leib ist mein Gedicht: Deutsche erotische Lyrik aus fünf Jahrhunderten*, ed. Heinz Ludwig Arnold (Bern/ München/ Wien: Rütten & Loening, 1970), 131.

These texts could only circulate in manuscript. Nowhere in the idealized aesthetics of eighteenth-century Germany was there an opening for the reception of such bawdy display. What might be displayed publicly then was only the regulated vision of the male, bodied as empowered and noble. Nevertheless, the guise of polite display did permit at least a utopian projection of an unabashed body to be shown and sustained, even if the foundations of physical being had to remain veiled. The possibility, however circumspectly uttered and carefully guarded, that one day he too might incorporate such an ideal was one source of Bürger's resistances. Although this vision of the emancipated male body may strike us today as itself repressive of other bodies, its revolutionary impact for the eighteenth century should not be denied. The radical implications of developing the body in public would return, elaborately, in the gymnastics movement in the German states of the early nineteenth-century.

But neither politically nor personally was Bürger to achieve in his lifetime the ideal of a body able to move and desire freely. The discrepancy between the powerlessness and immobility of a political subject and the aspirations of the lived body to be free and to move, to eat and drink, and to satisfy sexual desire, perforce led to crises, of which the French Revolution was not the least.[33]

---

[33] I am grateful to the Department of Romance Studies, Duke University, and especially to the Chairman, Dr. J.-J. Thomas, for accepting me as a visiting scholar and facilitating the completion of this essay.

Wanda Van Dusen

Reconciling Reason with Sensibility: Jakob Michael Reinhold Lenz's *Anmerkungen übers Theater*

LENZ'S 1774 ESSAY *ANMERKUNGEN ÜBERS THEATER* posits sensibility à la Rousseau against the eighteenth century imperative of reason in a way, which demonstrates how the Strom and Stress movement extended as well as opposed the Enlightenment. This is especially indicated by the speaker of the treatise, a subject reflecting within himself a lack of cohesion in resolving the split between rationality and emotionality. In discussing his topic, "the value of the theatrical spectacle" the often ironic, passionate speaker refuses the sober tutelage of Aristotelian aesthetics. "I have great respect for Aristotle, although not for his beard."[1] His denial of the authority of the *Poetics* also relates to what Judith Stiehm calls "our Aristotelian hangover", the separation of the senses from thought.[2]

Indeed without rejecting rationality itself, Lenz's speaker remains suspended between two discourses, personifying the mind/body split formulated in *De Anima*. "It remains then," writes Aristotle, "for the soul to enter [the body] and alone be divine."[3] As a result of granting dominance to neither side of the opposition, Lenz's essay presents a lack of systematically organized thought as well as a non-cohesive subject in the speaker. It reflects the Kantian "sublime" in its boundlessness, the movement which may be "compared to a vibration, i.e. to a quickly

---

[1] Jakob Michael Reinhold Lenz, *Werke und Schriften*, ed. Britta Titel und Hellmut Haug, (Stuttgart: Reclam, 1965), p. 234; translations are mine.

[2] Judith Hicks Stiehm, "The Unit of Political Analysis: Our Aristotelian Hangover," in: *Discovering Reality: Feminist Perspectives on Epistomology, Metaphysics, Methodology, and Philosophy of Science*, ed. Sandra Harding and Merrill B. Hintikka, (Boston: Reidel, 1983), p. 31.

[3] Lynda Lange, "Woman is Not a Rational Animal: On Aristotle's Biology of Reproduction," in: *Discovering Reality: Feminist Perspectives on Epistomology, Metaphysics, Methodology and Philosophy of Science*, op. cit., (736 b 29), p. 6.

alternating attraction toward and repulsion from the same object", "an abyss in which it [the imagination] fears to lose itself."[4]

Structurally, *Notes on the Theater* functions as a text within a text framed by the author's introduction. Presented as a talk, it has a performance-piece dimension meaning that the presence contained in the prose frame of the introduction opens on to another past, but dramatic presence.[5] Further complexity is added by the fact that the introduction is written in the third person plural, an authoritative, incorporating "we" voice. One might imagine an unnamed editor's having participated in the writing of it as well. The talk is actually thought to consist of several lectures given in Straßburg between 1771 and 1774 before the Societé de Philosophie et de Belles Lettres. This fact may partially explain the fragmentary character of the *Notes*.

However, the real reason is given in the last line of the short introductory paragraph, because it describes the speaker most provocatively and ambiguously as an "objective dilettant" ("ein unparteiischer Dilettant"). One may speculate here that this is in opposition mainly to the "man of science", i.e. the philosopher. Secondly, the content of the lecture is defined as his "uninhibited reasonings" ("ungehemmte Räsonnement"), something not well contained within form. Nor is the frame established by the introduction closed — the editor and/or author do not reappear at the end of the *Notes*, which further accentuates their open-ended quality. "[…] so," terminates the introduction, "we impart these remarks — if nothing else as the first uninhibited reasonings of an objective dilettant rhapsodically to our readers."[6] The reader is forewarned that this is not a neat, logically structured Enlightenment treatise. Its style and content aim at revealing the inadequacy of existing philosophical as well as literary conventions. The piece will be spoken "rhapsodically", that is to say as if an epic poem. Thus, the impasse between "rational" philosophy and "sensible" art is embodied in the style of the *Notes*, which in no way seek to resolve the conflict through systematized analysis.

The essay is therefore, a provocation against the argumentative forms of the Enlightenment, against Aristotelian aesthetics and French neo-classicism. Its rhetorical strategy militates for the Shakespearean cause of the Storm and Stress movement crystallized in the "cult of genius". By virtue of the creative impulse, the form of the *Notes* and the subjectivity of their speaker are pushed to the limit of the acceptable, toward "Folie". Lenz writes, "This we call enthusiasm, creativity, poetic ability or better, we don't name it at all". The "Genie" Shakespeare is

---

[4] Immanuel Kant, *Critique of Judgment:* First Book, "Analytic of the Beautiful," and Second Book, "Analytic of the Sublime"; in: *Critical Theory since Plato*, ed. Hazard Adams, (New York: Harcourt Brace Jovanovich, 1971), p. 395.

[5] Jacques Derrida, *De la grammatologie*, (Paris: Editions de Minuit, 1967), p. 439.

[6] Lenz, *Notes*, op. cit., p.329.

contrasted with the so-called "excellent worldly wise, the analysts, literally the 'dismemberers,' those who take the body apart, the critics, and all the other '-ers'" as Lenz calls them ("die Zergliederer, Kritiker").[7] His speaker proclaims, "We would like with one look to penetrate the inner nature of all beings, in one sensation to absorb and unite with ourselves all the bliss which is in nature."[8]

This explains the "present condition" ("der gegenwärtige Zustand") of the non-deductive lecturer, because inductive "cognition" ("Erkenntnis") in the genius is the equivalent of "all the seven senses" working together.[9] Thus, the language strongly, even erotically evokes the body, "[...] since my present condition and other accidental causes do not allow me to extend myself over my subject as widely, to penetrate it as deeply as I would like".[10] His style points to a central problem originating in Aristotle's concept of the rational soul as the organizer of matter, a concept later accentuated by the "Christian pastoral."[11] As Herder observed, " [...] in our culture, where reason often disqualifies emotion, and the artificial language of society stifles the sounds of nature." Herder therefore questions whether science and "cold conviction" "must determine everything."[12]

There is no doubt about the value of Aristotle's functionalist models coupled with the adversary Socratic method, which Nietzsche later terms the "nihilism" of scientific optimism.[13] Storm and Stress lives uncomfortably with Aristotle's claim that, "The rational soul may exist without the body, for no bodily activity has any connection with the activity of reason."[14] As a movement, it rejects the metaphors of Antiquity, which since the Renaissance had expressed the libidinal safely outside the parameters of Christianity.

Storm and Stress therefore, articulates the growing social and political crisis around definitions of reality posited by philosophical idealism and representations of reality offered by neo-classical art. Lenz's preference to leave the creative force "unnamed" expresses hesitation about committing it to any restraints of the symbolic field. The *Notes* are an attempt to expand the representational field beyond accepted norms via radical encounters with the imaginary, that is to say

---

[7] Lenz, *Notes*, op. cit., p. 336.

[8] Ibidem, p. 334.

[9] Ibidem, p. 336.

[10] Ibidem, p. 329.

[11] Michel Foucault, *L'Usage des Plaisir*, (Paris: Gallimard, 1984), p. 56.

[12] Johann Gottfried Herder, *Abhandlung über den Ursprung der Sprache*, ed. Hans Dietrich Irmscher, (Stuttgart: Reclam, 1966), p. 15 f.

[13] Friedrich Nietzsche, *Geburt der Tragödie*, in: *Werke in drei Bänden*, ed. Karl Schlechta, (München: Hanser, 1966), Vol I, p. 80 f.

[14] Quoted from Lynda Lange who cites *De Generatione Animalum*; p. 736.

the "un-nameable." Nevertheless in his "Geniestil", the speaker constructs a gigantic, imaginary theater upon which to parade actors from Greek antiquity through the 18th century, in order to show that the majority of the people receive little "edification" ("Erbauung") from the spectacles.[15] As a part of the Enlightenment himself, Lenz takes educating the spectator seriously. Unlike Herder who thought it possible to combine Italian comedy, Greek, French and English tragedy with German Drama into one repertoire, Lenz rejects all foreign theater but the Shakespearean. As a playwright preoccupied by aristocratic abuses and a reasoning bourgeoisie, he is a renewer of Lessing's middle class drama. Nevertheless in Lenz's opinion, only Shakespearean aesthetics can produce drama relevant to audiences by portraying the disparate and contradictory tendencies of the human soul. These fall outside Aristotle's poetics based on the harmonizing models of Sophocles.

Nature for Lenz is not primarily a domain of functional law discernable by reason and expressing universal principles. It is a realm of "multiplicity" ("Mannigfaltigkeit") within events and the characters themselves. In his essay of two years later, *On Change within the Theater in Shakespeare* (1776), Lenz proclaims that drama's value is to be found in the "interest" it creates for characters: "The great value of a dramatic composition always resides in stimulating interest, the portrayal of great and true characters and passions [...]."[16] Moreover, the philosophical principles present in Shakespeare's work, are at odds with Aristotelianism. These differences originate with Ockham (1290–1349), and the foundation of English empiricism in the Middle Ages. Ockhamism unintentionally undermined Aristotelian science by eliminating its Platonic universals and positing a theory of the particular. Truth, beauty, and goodness are henceforth first to be recognized in the singular, the individual.

Furthermore, Lenz negates the sequentiality of the Aristotelian rational soul, "[...] our soul desires whole heartedly to be successive neither in recognizing nor in desiring."[17] His plays illustrate this conflict in contexts of sexual seduction and class domination. In "The Soldiers" — written in the same year — the Countess, who is a model of aristocratic Enlightenment, reflects on the young Marie, ruined by a nobleman, "If I could discover something to combine her imagination with my intelligence [...]" (IV, 3). The play ends with the Magistrate's quite logical proposal of a brothel for the King's army to protect middle class girls from seduction by aristocratic officers. The self-sacrifice of these prostitutes, termed "Amazons" in the scene, would preserve social harmony. At the end of the

---

[15] Lenz, *Notes*, op. cit., p. 330.

[16] Ibidem, p. 322.

[17] Ibidem, p. 334.

Magistrates's exposition, the Countess comments, "How little men know the hearts and desires of women." (V, 5)

Similarly, Läuffer in "The Tutor" finds no unifying religious or philosophical discourse to resolve the mind/body conflict. As is the tendency in Lessing's dramas, this character turns the violence of the libidinal and social issues on himself. Läuffer's self-castration is an indication that the modern hero's subjectivity resides in a willingness to accept a maimed existence rather than defeat or triumph in death.[18] It marks a crisis in the Enlightenment subject, whom Fredric Jameson describes as "the autonomous bourgeois monad."[19] Läuffer exemplifies the deeply historical phenomenon of the reification and separation of the senses in modern times."[20] He is a catastrophic commentary on the Kantian notion of an age of majority ("Mündigkeit") based on independent thinking and free actions.

In the *Notes*, this crisis in subjectivity is crystallized by the metaphor of Deianira's poisoned shirt, which occupies a powerful position at the end of the essay when the speaker presents his translation of Shakespeare, "[...] may he still appear, my Hercules, even if in the shirt of Deianira —"[21] This is more than an expression of doubt about a translation which could do damage to the Shakespearean cause or about the "Genie" himself criticized by people like Wieland as "ungrammatical and formless."[22] It is a figure, which expresses a divided subject intensely ambivalent himself about the unresolved struggle between reason and sensibility. Deianira's shirt expresses all of the pain inherent in the modern sublime as formulated by Kant. "The feeling of the sublime is [...] a feeling of pain arising from a want of accordance between the aesthetic estimation of magnitude formed by the imagination and the estimation of the same formed by reason."[23] As *Notes on the Theater* indicates, much of modern beauty will henceforth found itself in the discordant, sensual sublime rather than a contemplation of the good in the beautiful ideal.

The *Note's* loose associative form reveals deliberate ruptures in representation marked by recurrent ellipsis, broken syntax erratically placed questions and

---

[18] Peter Szondi, *Die Theorie des bürgerlichen Trauerspiels im 18. Jahrhundert*, ed. Gert Mattenklott, (Frankfurt am Main: Suhrkamp, 1973), p. 186.

[19] Fredric Jameson, *Postmodernism or the Cultural Logic of Late Capitalism*, (Durham: Duke University Press, 1991), p. 15.

[20] Ibidem, p. 253.

[21] Lenz, *Notes*, op. cit., p. 362.

[22] Eva Maria Inbar, *Shakespeare in Deutschland: Der Fall Lenz*, (Tübingen: Niemeyer, 1982), p. 24.

[23] Immanuel Kant, *From 'Critique of Judgement'*, trans J.H. Bernard, in: *Critical Theory since Plato*, ed. Hazard Adams, (New York: Harcourt Brace Jovanovich, 1971), p. 395.

exclamations. The subject so frees himself from rhetorical convention as to be in danger of fragmentation and of shattering the common system of communication linking him to his listeners.[24] He is often at the limit of coherent discourse, where to speak with Derrida, words become more a "poison" than a "remedy".[25] There is an unwillingness to establish continuity either via logical argumentation or by way of a consistent narrative line. This deprives the *Notes* of a discursive solid ground and signals the "disconnection" between the discourses of art and philosophy at the centre of Storm and Stress.[26]

After "nailing together" his stage upon which to review the history of European theater, the speaker interrupts his monologue to mention his "goal" ("Endzweck"). "With your permission, I will begin a bit far back, because my goal — my goal? What do you think it could be?" Authority is passed from the speaker to his listeners, and throughout the delivery of the lecture the goal is only mentioned as a retardative device, an absent presence creating unfulfilled expectation. It is even suggested that the listeners themselves may accidentally discover the goal, the consequences of which however would remain vague and undefined. "Perhaps you will if you have ridden off with me — come across it yourselves and then — ."[27]

This strategy is designed to disorganize any audience's need for definitive, "closed" meanings. Such elliptical constructions typical of Storm and Stress occur repeatedly and suggest the isolation of a subject caught in a kaleidoscopic multiplication of perspectives and pressures. Lenz's assaults on cohesiveness are calculatedly radical and correspond to his own "open" dramatic form.[28] In 'The Tutor", the Major expresses violently opposed thoughts in a moment of intense shame and psychic conflict after rescuing his socially ruined daughter from suicide by drowning. "(He lifts her in his arms) There girl — I should go back to the pond with you — (swinging her toward the pond) but we don't want to go swimming before we've learned to swim." (IV, 5)

Unlike Herder, who saw Shakespeare's tragic hero's as determined by their historical situation, Lenz detaches characterization from both the fateful machinations of history and any philosophical universals.[29] Being based on both reason and sensibility Lenz's position is dual, if not ultimately paralysing. On the other

---

[24] Cf. Fritz Martini, "Die Poetik des Dramas im Sturm und Drang," in: *Deutsche Dramentheorie*, Vol I. ed. Reinhold Grimm, (Frankfurt/Main: Athenäum, 1971).

[25] Jaques Derrida, *De la grammatologie*, (Paris: Editions de Minuit, 1967), p. 78 f.

[26] Cf. Philippe Lacoue-Labarthe and Jean-Luc Nancy, *The Literary Absolute*, trans. Philip Bernard and Cheryl Lester, (Albany: State University Press of New York Press, 1988), p. 30.

[27] Lenz, *Notes*, op. cit., p. 332.

[28] Volker Klotz, *Geschlossene und offene Form im Drama*, (München: Hanser, 1969), p. 171.

[29] Cf. Fritz Martini, "Die Poetik des Dramas im Sturm und Drang", op. cit., p. 154.

hand, there is respect for causality, "We hate plots whose causes we don't understand and have nothing to do with them." On the other hand, following Shakespeare's example, Lenz locates these causes in the characters themselves, who create their own events, who independently and unfailingly keep the whole device going themselves, without needing the gods in the clouds or anything else."[30]

In opposition again to Aristotle, Lenz insists that the human being is more important than his or her fate. The Greeks of the classical period wanted to see exemplary fates played out. This reflected perhaps a greater social unity of a polis-based on male aristocratic citizenship to the exclusion of women and slaves. In Lenz's theater, the public comes to see "a series of actions" ("eine Reihe von Handlungen") which psychologically portray the characters in their specificity. The characters are as isolated socially as are the scenes within the plays, and they speak past each other in dialogues which are deliberately commonplace and unquotable. Ultimately, the organizing principle of these strings of actions are "counterpoint and equivalent,"[31] not metaphysical absolutes. In criticizing what he calls "today's Aristotelians" Lenz asks, "These gentlemen may be great philosophers with great general human insight, laws for knowing the human soul, but where is the individual in all that?"[32]

Interest in the characters replaces the three unities of time, place, and action which serve as mere "decoration." To emphasize how confining such rules are for the dramatist, the speaker of the *Notes* flaunts the claim that he has not even entirely read the *Poetics*. Its rules domesticate theater, which should depict the world. "If you are comfortable, gentlemen, limiting yourselves to the dimensions of one house and one day, in God's name, keep your family dramas, your miniature portraits and leave us our world."[33]

It is Lenz's demand for a rendering of the particular which most distinguishes his work. For example, Lessing allows for individual speculation only as long as it is guided by the universal of virtue, "[...] virtue, because of its eternal blissful consequences."[34] However, as a basis for dramatizing the human personality, Lenz rejects such axioms, because like references to deities they result in "marionettes" on stage. Lessing observes, "In nature, [...] everything crisscrosses everything, everything exchanges with everything [...]. However, this endless

---

[30] Lenz, *Notes*, op. cit., p. 343.

[31] Jürgen Zenke, "Das Drama des Sturm und Drang," in: *Handbuch des deutschen Dramas*, ed. Walter Hinck, (Düsseldorf: Bagel, 1980), p. 132.

[32] Lenz, *Notes*, op. cit., p. 341.

[33] Ibidem, p. 344.

[34] Gotthold Ephraim Lessing, *Die Erziehung des Menschengeschlechtes*, (Stuttgart: Reclam, 1965), p. 27.

multiplicity serves only as a spectacle for a human mind."[35] Consequently, Lessing's "aesthetics of effect" ("Wirkungsästhetik") arranges actions to produce pity and fear in the spectator, "In a word, this fear is pity applied to ourselves," leading to an understanding of virtue.[36]

To Lenz, such constructs are "mechanical" in the traditional Aristotelian way and exclude a large part of psychological and social reality for the sake of an idealized world view concentrated in terms like "virtue" or "beautiful nature." The lecturer of the *Notes* declares, "The true poet does not compose in his imagination as he pleases that, which you gentlemen like to call beautiful nature, but which with your permission is nothing other than missed nature."[37] This is the equivalent of Lessing's imposing order on the multiple spectacle of nature with "a mind." "Beautiful nature" is an abstraction "missing" what nature really is in its particularity. Lenz's playwright can only choose a "perspective" ("ein Standpunkt") and then produce in an empirical way what is perceived.

This is a call for realism in art and philosophy, which is later taken up by Büchner, who argues that nature cannot be comprehended by its laws and purposive movements alone, "Nature does not function according to goals, it does not consume itself in an endless series of goals, one determining the other; rather nature is in all of its expressions immediately self-satisfying."[38] This non-hierarchical, non-purposive view is related to Büchner's theatrical representations of the working class protagonist. His is a holistic vision, which incorporates all the so-called natural and social aberations.

Kant, in the *Critique of Judgement*, posited man as "the only being which has the purpose of its existence in itself [...]." Storm and Stress aesthetics departs from Kant where he claims that man "can determine his purpose by reason."[39] Lenz's work, like that of the later avant-gardes of modernity, is linked to the notion of the sublime as formulated by Kant, "Sublimity [...] does not reside in anything of nature, but only in our mind, insofar as we can become conscious that we are superior to nature within, and therefore also to nature without [...]."[40] Lenz's plays and essays tend to dissolve the distinction between inside and outside and demonstrate that the mind's tactics to govern the body's drives may exact a terrible price. Character is thus a totality of rational and irrational traits forming the centre of drama.

---

[35] Gotthold Ephraim Lessing, "Die Hamburgische Dramaturgie," *Lessings Werke*, ed. Kurt Wölfel, (Frankfurt: Insel, 1967), p. 557.

[36] Ibidem, 75, 579.

[37] Lenz, *Notes*, op. cit., p. 336.

[38] Georg Büchner, *Werke und Briefe*, (München: Deutscher Taschenbuchverlag, 1988), p. 269.

[39] Kant, *Critique of Judgement*, op. cit., p. 389.

[40] Ibidem, p. 396.

While comedies have a cause as their focal point, the total person is at the centre of tragedy. Like Lenz's tragi-comedies, they therefore do not tolerate "torn out" plots ("abgerissene Handlungen").[41] The speaker asks, "Are we to blame that we no longer enjoy plots torn out of events but are old enough to want the total picture? [...] or do you shy away, gentlemen, from seeing a human being?"[42] Confining the subject to the categories of rationality reduces nature to "mere objectivity." The cost of this is an increasing sense of alienation from that which is objectified, including the self and other human beings. According to Horkheimer and Adorno, this is how "Enlightenment behaves toward things as a dictator toward men."[43]

In the *Notes*, Lenz militates against unity imposed from above by a tradition described as "so little German in tone, so critically quivering, so beautifully accomplished — whoever has ears for that let him clap, the people are confounded!"[44] However, that the lower classes play no central role in his plays indicates how much a part of the Enlightenment Lenz in fact was. His vision of a national middle class theater integrating reason and sensibility has greater social and political implications than he himself arrives at formulating. *Notes on the Theater* remains militant but unprogrammatic, if not paralysed in utopianism. "What does that mean, the three unities, I want to give you a hundred unities, which all remain however one. Unity of nation, unity of language, unity of religion, unity of customs — [...] the poet and the audience must feel the one unity but not classify."[45] Lenz is writing within twenty years of the French Revolution when the class conflicts provoking Läuffer's self-mutilation will find violent political expression.

---

[41] Lenz, *Notes*, op. cit., p. 361.

[42] Ibidem, p. 345.

[43] Max Horkheimer and Theodor Adorno, *Dialectic of Enlightenment*, trans. John Cumming, (New York: Herder & Herder, 1972), p. 9.

[44] Lenz, *Notes*, op. cit., p. 332.

[45] Ididem, p. 334 f.

Wulf Koepke

Mephisto and Aesthetic Nihilism

THERE IS NO FAUST WITHOUT MEPHISTO.[1] Mephisto, it has been maintained, is the real tragic hero of Goethe's great allegory of human destiny within the realm of cosmic forces. This may stretch the term "tragic" too far, but an aura of inevitable futility (if not doom) surrounds this most fascinating character that comes close enough to tragedy — as close as modern civilization permits. Given the complexities of Mephisto's character, and the fascination of evil in modern times, it is more than surprising that scholarly attention paid to Mephisto is scant, especially when compared to the enormous scholarly energy spent on Goethe's *Faust* as a whole.[2] Mephisto's first self-definition: "Ein Teil von jener Kraft, / Die stets das Böse will und stets das Gute schafft" has been taken literally, although Faust calls it a "Rätselwort." Mephisto is, of course, not always believable; if the name means anything, it is probably "deceiver" or "liar." But if Mephisto "schafft das Gute," the world is indeed in harmony, Faust's compact with the devil is only beneficial, and the devil is truly God's "Knecht." There are reasons to doubt such reassuring views. Not only does Faust often seem "das Gute zu wollen und das Böse zu schaffen," he also appears to Mephisto at least at one point to be "so ziemlich eingeteufelt," the "Nachspiel im Himmel" that saves Faust's "Unsterbliches" has to come as a real surprise: he is saved mostly in spite of himself.

But again, it would not be possible either to present this world as dualistic. Goethe's *Faust* is a document of an age that was convinced it had moved beyond the mere opposition of good and evil. In this context the figure of Mephisto is a disquieting element, not so much because it preserves many elements of the traditional devil lore, but because of its less obvious modernity. It has been observed that with the growing civilisatory refinement of the ages, the devil as the incarnation of evil, also became more refined, more civilized, and thus less pernicious.[3] While the first part of the statement is true, the conclusion that the devil might do less harm in a more refined manner, may be sadly mistaken. With the

---

[1] Maximilian Rudwin, *The Devil in Legend and Literature*, (Chicago: The Open Court Publishing Co., 1931), p. 188ff.

[2] Cf. Günther Mahal, *Mephistos Metamorphosen. Fausts Partner als Repräsentant literarischer Teufelsgestaltung*, (Göppingen: Kümmerle, 2nd ed., 1982), for a survey.

[3] Maximilian Rudwin, op. cit., among others, argues along this line.

refinement comes, most of all, a growing talent to deceive. While the devil with horns is descending into the realm of the burlesque, evil begins to take new and unexpected shapes.

The consensus among scholars on the history of the devil that the rationalism of the eighteenth century meant the disappearance of devil mythology, needs to be reexamined.[4] What actually happened was quite different. First of all, "superstitions" as the age called them, never died out. On the contrary, they seemed to thrive in the shadow of the belief in reason. What actually changed was public policy and the role of the Christian churches, and that was indeed a momentous event. The pervasive belief of the Protestant and Catholic church hierarchies in the existence of a kingdom of hell with thousands of devils and their messenger spirits, of magic powers being a major tool of diabolic deception and seduction, had led to unending persecutions of sorcerers and witches, a general atmosphere of suspicion, even fear and terror and a legal system that sanctioned brutal punishments in order to purify Christianity and save humanity from evil. It is understandable that such atmosphere favoured the expression of hatred and resentment of "others," and many unrelated private animosities went into such accusations of possession by the devil.

The eighteenth century can be credited with the gradual abolition of such practices, and the conviction that suspicious phenomena belonged primarily to the jurisdiction of medicine and not theology. Spirits and magic were declared illusionary, and human behaviour attributed to inner drives and forces. Ideally, the human being would be self-responsible, and if a person misbehaved and proved to be harmful for society, this needed to be punished in order to protect other people and maintain order. Crimes were not in the mind, such as evil thoughts, but only actions, murder, theft, or assault, could be punishable.

Whereas church inquisition and techniques at witches' trials had developed a remarkable sophistication in ferreting out evil thoughts and connections with evil powers, real or imagined, the psychology of the age of tolerance began to move in the opposite direction, that is, to look for motifs or circumstances that might excuse, even exonerate crimes and criminals. The subjective factor in the administration of justice began to swing into the defendants' favour.

This was only plausible for society, since the notion of evil was attacked vigorously. The long debate about the existence of the devil, especially in the Lutheran church,[5] that ended with the victory of the "progressive" party, did not really replace the devil with the notion of evil. It changed the notion of evil itself. *Le mal* in Leibniz' theodicy and in the many philosophers and theologians

---

[4] This point is made from Gustav Roskopf, *Geschichte des Teufels*, (1869) to Jeffrey Burton Russel, *Mephistopheles. The Devil in the Modern World*, (Ithaca/London: Cornell University Press, 1986).

[5] Cf. Karl Aner, *Die Theologie der Lessingzeit*, (Halle/Saale: Niemeyer, 1929).

expanding on his arguments, was imperfection, *Mangel*, a purely negative attribute, even in a mathematical sense, the lack of something, whereas the good was equated with plenitude, life forces, thriving, and higher development. It is no accident that the German term for the pivotal concept perfection and its derivative perfectibility, was *Vollkommenheit* resp. *Vervollkommnung* which contained the ingredient "voll." With this new schema, a sliding scale, as it were, from void to plenitude, instead of irreconcilable opposites, such as good and evil, the inevitable phenomenon of death took on new meaning.[6] This disturbing element in its brutal and often seemingly senseless occurrences, had to be integrated into the order of life forces in order to justify the new world view. Death had to be redefined as metamorphosis, as rebirth, usually called by the theologically acceptable word palingenesis.

It was not anymore, in this life- and development-oriented world view, the fear of eternal damnation and torture that haunted anxious souls; but the thought that death might not be just a transition, it could be the ultimate end, annihilation. It was disturbing enough to consider materialistic heresies as possible which would imply that, as reality consisted only of matter, the death of a person meant the disintegration into organic particles, and the end of a person's identity. But it would be even worse to think that everything around us, even we ourselves, were just figments of our imagination, provoked by the senses, and thus void of substantiality. Following the Kantian revolution, of course, substance became irrelevant and was displaced by function; but people were not quite ready to accept this bracketing out of "das Ding an sich" psychologically. The fear of nothingness, reinforced by the perspective of an ever expanding universe which may indeed be a vacuum, found many modes of expression.

One of these modes was the devil. While the devil was purged from legal codes and church language, he or she reentered with new vigour the realm of creative imagination. This shift of devil mythology from theology to fiction and artistic imagination is an easily observable fact. It is usually attributed to nascent Romanticism (or pre-Romanticism) but it happens within the later stages of enlightenment. This point is muddled by the messy terminology of periodization, especially in the German tradition. And there is no doubt that, among the many fascinating devil figures of that age, Goethe's Mephistopheles stands out, linked to one of the most potent modern myths, that of Faust, and recreated by one of the great writers of all ages, Goethe. This does not mean, however, that all attention should be focused on Mephisto, as the one and only embodiment of the devil.[7] On the contrary, the variety of devil figures is enormous. It is, or course,

---

[6] For a survey that needs to be updated, cf. Walther Rehm, *Der Todesgedanke in der deutschen Dichtung vom Mittelalter bis zur Romantik*, (Tübingen: Niemeyer, 1967).

[7] The vast literature on Romanticism is the key to the definition of other devil myths created or shaped in modern times, e.g. the figures connected with Don Juan.

not assumed here, that it was only in the eighteenth century when the devil entered the realm of fiction. That statement would be so blatantly absurd it only needs to be mentioned to be discarded. But it remains that previous literary creations have to be seen in a certain theological framework. Klopstock's *Messias*, trying to outdo Milton, presents a curious transition, creating a contrite devil, Abbadona who would like to shed his devilish nature, but is unable to liberate himself from the evil within.

Goethe recreated an old myth that, in the sixteenth century, had been refashioned to fit the post-Reformation frame of mind, albeit in a slightly subversive manner. In the 1587 book on *Doktor Faustus* that may have had oral precursors, the messenger from hell is called Mephostophiles. He is not really a devil, but a messenger spirit who needs authorization from the hierarchy for all major decisions and ventures. This spirit is promptly on the scene when Faust battles attacks of melancholy (we might call it depression), and fits the description of the "melancholical devil" in the "devil books" of the *Theatrum Diabolorum*. A devil named Mephostophiles has not been found in the literature prior to 1587; but the popularity of the *Volksbuch* prompted an expanded use of the name, beyond fiction. Here was the case of a literary devil entering into "real" devil lore.

Mephostophiles acts as Faust's servant, reluctantly at times, and is persuasive, sarcastic, cold, menacing, whatever the situation demands. It would be too much to say that he develops his own personality. There is no comparison with established figures such as Lucifer or Satan. This really works to Mephisto's (as Goethe called him, following a later version) advantage: he can be shaped, physically and mentally, by the individual writer and artist; and it appealed to quite a few writers to leave an air of indistinctness.

Goethe was originally intent on recreating the Renaissance ambience from which the Faust myth originated; that would have mandated a full hierarchy of hell. But such plans, traces of which are preserved in the Walpurgis Night, were displaced by the modern turn the story took, especially with the introduction of Gretchen. However, with the historical garb of the Renaissance, Goethe also retained quite a few attributes and paraphernalia of the folklore surrounding the devil. And yet, a curious transformation occurred. Originally the *Knittelvers*, quoting, as it were, the puppet play of *Doktor Faustus* and writers like Hans Sachs, introduced some ironic distance between these old myths and modern sophistication, but then, the *Knittelvers*, under Goethe's talented hands, acquired a new dignity, without however, losing its folksiness, and Mephisto emerged from behind the ridiculous folklore as a very complex and sophisticated character. Quoting and making fun of a previous naïve age allowed more irony directed against the present. Whereas Faust regresses from the book learning to the use of magic power, instead of advancing to the new science of observation, with or without the help of instruments (a process that concerned Goethe very deeply), Mephisto moves freely from magic tricks to modern experiments. He is condescending enough to play the Protestant devil who provides magic and supernatural help merely as an illusion for the victim, and he admits, enlightened intellectual that he is, that he is somewhat ashamed of such tricks, he does it for the sake of the credulous people. As a matter of fact, medieval magic and alchemy turns directly into modern magic and alchemy, as is exemplified by many incidents of the second part of *Faust*. Mephisto, however, does not only bridge the gap from "pre-scientific" to scientific (or "post-scientific"?) attitudes and experiments, he also represents a cold rationalism that sees through all of these games and considers them ludicrous. Maybe Mephisto has, as a fallen angel, an ideal of perfection that is unattainable. In any event, in his massive negativity, he can see only the futility of all imperfect thriving and efforts that will end up in ridiculous failures. Thus, while his irresistible urge is to destroy, to annihilate, most of the human and historical events in which he participates, are for him nothing but games void of substance. Life is *ein Spiel*, and Mephisto keeps reminding the audience that it is, and that he is not duped by any optimistic cover-up. Mephisto, in the economy of the play *Faust*, assumes the role of both director and commentator. He directs the "shows" imbedded in the play, and he participates in all the illusions and delusions that occur on different levels in *Faust*. Not that the play ever goes according to his plans: he is always confronted with surprises from the different actors.

Mephisto therefore wears his mask of traditional paraphernalia and magic powers like a costume, and he lifts the mask whenever it suits him. On the stage, Mephisto is invariably portrayed with the appearance of the traditional devil. But would it not be appropriate that not only Gretchen, but also the audience has some doubts about who he really is? The modern devil is well disguised, not recognizable from the outside. He or she looks like most of us, only more fascinating, more intelligent, and many times more handsome and beautiful. While in Goethe's play, the devil is "properly" introduced as the devil, the first scenes are surrounded by enough irony to warrant the doubt: is this devil playing man, or man playing the devil? Or a creature of Faust's inner demons? Mephisto likes uncertainties and deception. He should not be that easily recognizable. But then, a devil in the old costume looks more harmless, even ridiculous, and this may be one motivation behind the theatre practice.

The mixture of old and new is typical, of course, for the entire play, especially for the figure of Faust who, in spite of being hailed or condemned as the embodiment of "modern man," (which is still better than being the "eternal German") carries a heavy baggage of the past, setting up Goethe's larger view on history, and in the second part, on nature, myth, humankind, and the march of times. None of this can be discussed here, although it would be pertinent. Mephisto is involved in all of this, and his role should be properly acknowledged.

In the case of Mephisto, the manner of quoting the tradition of devil lore is significant. While Mephisto dazzles Faust with his magical fireworks, and dazzles the audience with his brilliant wit and his cold irony, he carries the melancholy of the melancholical devil from 1587 into the modern text. Underneath the theatricality of play producing and of verbal craftiness, Mephisto contemplates "das ewig Leere," which he likes, as he says, on the one hand, but this attempted annihilation, *Vernichtung*, of life itself that is the sombre subtext of all exploits and Faustian deeds undermined and subverted by Mephisto, is somewhat uncanny for Mephisto himself. He may be the devil, or the devil's messenger thriving on the weakness offered by Faust's melancholy and midlife crisis, but in diverting Faust from his depression, Mephisto seems also to divert himself. It is imaginable to consider the devil the prey of melancholy himself, as he contemplates the futility of every effort, including his own, and the infinite emptiness of the universe. In Goethe's (and Herder's) cosmos, negativity and its melancholy are self-destructive. Evil limits itself through such destructive (i.e. self-destructive) forces, and has to remain inferior to life-sustaining and expanding *Kraft*; but Faust's career is not a very good proof of this, it rather indicates that he cannot get active except with Mephisto's destructive help that subverts his good intentions.

We don't have to believe Mephisto when he says that he pities the human race, but while Faust seems "eingeteufelt" in the course of his association with Mephisto, Mephisto appears more human (but not less evil). It is not necessary to belabour the point that Mephisto served as a reference point for subsequent evil figures of the nineteenth and twentieth centuries. It bears emphasizing, however, that Mephisto is a transitional figure on several accounts. He makes fun of the traditional hell, but inspires the anxiety of the *nihil*, the absolute annihilation and emptiness. He also is a spirit, maybe an elemental spirit who has entered the human realm and becomes almost human. The subsequent devil figures, if they are not emanations of the psyche, are human beings with an aura of a curse. They are attractive through a melancholical beauty and intelligence, and the inescapable boredom of hopelessness that inspires them to destructive diversions. In later developments of Romanticism, it seems as if beauty and superior knowledge can only be granted by such destructive forces that, in the end, have to turn against themselves. Falling prey to the temptation of evil is not punished by torture in hell, but by extinction, as the moral and metaphysical nihilism would decree it. The aesthetic game of beauty and pleasure may be nothing but varnish over this doomsday scenario.

If one searches the eighteenth century for the seeds for such radical views, they were present, but carefully repressed. They emerged in debates on atheism, solipsism, or materialism. If God did not exist or did not guarantee the reality of the cosmos and the superiority of spiritual life forces over inertia and destruction, the universe would be fragmented, perceptions would be arbitrary and uncertain, and the artist could not be a second maker, but only an entertainer, a provider of illusions as diversions. If Faust represents at one level the artist with his creative powers, Mephisto as well does very much what the *Theaterdirektor* had demanded in the *Vorspiel*: he provides a good show for the masses to divert attention from the real drama and to alleviate the existential boredom.

Faust and Mephisto demonstrate not only the limitations of human endeavour and the underlying anxiety of the human condition, in a more specific way, they demonstrate the limits and dangers of Enlightenment and the death of the devil. The devil declared as non-existent, takes cover and reappears in different guises and disguises, sometimes masquerading as the old devil himself. Quoting, as it were, the old belief in the devil, and hiding behind the enlightened belief that the devil is nothing but an outgrown superstition, Mephisto takes the viewer and reader from the pre-enlightened age to a post-enlightenment age where the demons are allowed free reign since they remain unrecognized. In terms of the history of culture and literature, the devil is chased out of the church (one could even say out of the kingdom of hell); as an exile, he or she wanders away from diabology and into anthropology: the devil takes the shape of human beings, especially the intellectual, the commentator, the pessimist, the *l'art pour l'art* artist, the worshipper of beauty and pleasure. While the dichotomies of good and evil are still being manipulated for the ideological myths of a political and propagandist nature, the true fascination of evil has migrated into the aesthetic sphere where humans endowed with superhuman evil powers dominate the scene. This is evident in the infantile popular literature scene, but it derives from the dark side of Romanticism and its fascination with evil beauty. Since the arts, freed from the service of churches and monarchs, have become largely a luxury, rather than a necessity, in life, their freedom is less limited, and they are not taken seriously. If the devil had wanted to survive and manifest himself without being seriously attacked, this had to be an optimal hiding place.

Mephisto, it was stated above, became the most popular modern devil, and paved the way for the romantic human devils. But every major German writer of the period of Goethe wrestled with the problem of evil and the proclaimed death of the devil — let alone popular novels and plays, especially the "gothic" variety. It is useful to demonstrate this with at least one example. I chose Jean Paul Richter, especially since he is hardly ever mentioned in the history of devil figures. I could have used Klinger, Tieck, E.T.A. Hoffmann (of course), the earlier Schiller, Kleist, among others.

Among Richter's early satires is a scene where the devil demonstrates during a masked ball that he does not really exist. This piece was never published, but it went through three different versions,[8] the last one conveying the existential experience of nothingness. Jean Paul's text focuses on the enlightened view of

---

[8] A detailed analysis with the theological antecedents is given in Friedrich Wilhelm Biggemann, *Maschine und Teufel. Jean Pauls Jugendsatiren nach ihrer Modellgeschichte*, (Freiburg/Br.: Alber, 1975).

people that the devil does not exist, and makes fun of it; but at this point, he is not really interested in the powers of evil. Similarly, the flimsy fiction of *Die Auswahl aus des Teufels Papieren* (1789) seems superimposed on a very diverse collection of short texts, mostly satires. The introduction says that Hasus, the deceased author, was such a good person that he could not have possibly written such nasty and evil satires. Therefore, the devil possessed him and during the night, used his body as a *Schreibmaschine* (a first case of automatic writing?). Satires, for the bourgeois world were destructive, devilish texts making fun of sacred virtues and institutions. Hasus, in his own introduction, describes the horrors of solipsism.

In his treatise on poetics, the *Vorschule der Ästhetik* (1804), Jean Paul would distinguish between satire and humour, and then, he would also distinguish devilish laughter from true humour. If Hasus is truly the victim of the devil and talks with a foreign voice, like a ventriloquist, his decent human character is perverted. (Richter, the satirist spoke of course ironically). It is indicative that seductive evil, in Jean Paul's works, is connected with masked balls, and with imitation. There is an evil ventriloquist in *Titan* who haunts Schoppe and is one of the causes of his final insanity, but the ultimate scenes are those of Roquairol, the real human devil, who is imitating Albano's voice during the night in order to seduce Linda; and who then kills himself on the stage playing himself in a play written by himself, his death followed by an epilogue spoken by the evil ventriloquist. Roquairol who has seductive charm (and impressed the German romantics) is a role player and imitator who needs the diversion of new roles to escape boredom. He also needs more and more sophisticated pleasures and evil machinations to satisfy his needs, and he ultimately acts out of revenge against the more fortunate Albano. In his last novel, *Der Komet*, Jean Paul introduced a strange figure, the *Ledermensch*, as the real antagonist to the imagined prince Nikolaus Marggraf who lives in a world of illusions and delusions, made possible through his invention of artificial diamonds. The *Ledermensch* embodies the power and dangers of imagination: He imagined himself to be evil, and thus became the servant of the devil (or so he thinks); he speaks alternately with two voices, one childlike innocent voice, and the voice of evil. Imagining evil, he became the vessel of evil powers. The fragmentary novel breaks off with a scene where the *Ledermensch* confesses his sins and condition, and threatens to attack Marggraf. Imagination, the creative power, can also be the power of evil creating its own world in its own image, disregarding God's universe, substituting human artifice for God's nature.

The world is not a given, but a universe of forces waiting to be shaped in different ways. With notions like action and creation becoming central for the discourse on the human condition, the idea of a remaking of God's world in the human image becomes more commonplace, and for many anxious souls, this means a diabolic counter-creation. The seeds for such a concept are, again, evident in Goethe's *Faust*, especially in the second part where Mephisto, like Faust, evolves in new ways. He is seen here as involved in modern economy, especially the illusion of wealth created by paper money, in technology, he subverts the reshaping of the map through the creation of new land from the sea, and he is associated with warfare as well, be it at the command of Faust or by himself. He does not invent, but he directs and subverts the original plan. Above all, Mephisto is in many ways involved with processes of the arts and artistic theories. What he had to offer, certainly benefitted the writers and writers of Romanticism. Whereas the end of *Faust* leaves no doubt about the hopeful outlook, other voices at the time and later were lamenting the powers of deception masking the self-destruction of aesthetic pleasures. The aesthetic pleasures of pain and destruction (sadism), connected with cold irony and sarcastic intellectualism, became the trademark of this despair over an incurable world, the hopelessness of true pessimism. While at first such views seemed to be the devil's advocate rather than the devil's own voice, this difference between the devil's advocate who wants to warn, and the devil's messenger who seduces, became blurred.

The eighteenth century liberated the devil from the captivity in the churches, to be freely available in the arts, literature, politics, and any type of propagandist myth. There is a dialectical connection between the use of the devil icon for the absolute negative that one wants to destroy, and the totally amoral character of the modern aesthetic devil. Eliminating the concept of an independent evil that does not serve the good, the eighteenth century endangered the notion of good as well, as the distinctions became increasingly arbitrary. The notion of good has become an instrumental utilitarian category. The figure of the devil, however, is a last reminder of the power of absolutes, even when their existence is denied. In this context, Mephisto is the great embodiment of this enormous ambiguity: the memory of a devil in whom we humans do not believe, but who demonstrates his powers in unexpected ways. Although Mephisto is a most troubling figure, standing between the previous evil spirits and the modern evil humans, affirming and denying the progress of enlightenment at the same time, he has been taken for granted to a large degree, as a mere contrast to the figure of Faust. It would be foolish to pretend, however, that we already know everything about Mephisto and what he has done to the world during the last two centuries.

Thomas Salumets

Pleasures of Influence: Goethe, Bloom, Elias[1]

DURING THE SO CALLED *GENIEZEIT* the word "originality" gained increased significance in discourses on poetic, artistic, philosophical, scientific and political visions of progress.[2] For those drawn into these discourses, "originality" was, and still is, a source of intense yet vague anxieties — anxieties which continue to be self-inflicted. With this paper I aim to contribute to a more productive, less anxiety ridden understanding of the word "originality".

The methodological anatomy of this paper takes its shape above all from the work of the social theorist Norbert Elias (1897-1990) on the "civilizing process". The particular vista adopted here is perhaps most adequately described as "gathered thinking" — a cognitive mode that, in short, attributes foremost epistemic value to synthesis rather than analysis.[3]

The argument rests upon the assumption that it is not useful to frame discussions of "originality" in "terms of a static polarity between total 'objectivity' and total 'subjectivity'."[4] Such teleologically inspired discussions perpetuate the myth of the artistic (or, for that matter, any) self as "creator" rather than tip the balance towards a discussion of "originality" less determined by our inclination towards egocentrism.

Going hand in hand with egocentrism, with our desire for the everlasting is a corresponding degree of anxiety — or as Milan Kundera put it: "Man reckons

---

[1] The article is based on a paper delivered at the *Eight International Congress on the Enlightenment*, University of Bristol, 21–27 July 1991.

[2] Cf. Thomas Salumets, "Unterwanderte 'Normendestruktion': Zur Poetologie des Sturm-und-Drang-Drames," in: *Euphorion* 85.1 (1991), p. 70–84.

[3] Cf. Karl-Siegbert Rehberg's assessment of Elias' way of thinking: "Alle in diesem Aufsatz genannten Aspekte der auf Norbert Elias wirkenden Einflußbeziehungen ließen sich auch pejorativ mißverstehen oder — wozu Elias selbst neigt — als Eklektizismusvorwurf lesen. Das ist ein Einwand ohne Belang, denn ich glaube, daß alle vorwärtstreibenden Entwürfe Verknüpfungen sind, Zusammenfassungen beinhalten und Fortsetzungen darstellen." Karl-Siegbert Rehberg, "Form und Prozeß. Zu den katalysatorischen Wirkungschancen einer Soziologie aus dem Exil: Norbert Elias," in: *Materialien zu Norbert Elias' Zivilisationstheorie*, ed. Peter Gleichmann, Johan Goudsblom, Hermann Krote, (Frankfurt/M: Suhrkamp, 1982), p. 154f.

[4] Stephen Mennell, *Norbert Elias: Civilization and the Human Self-Image*, (Oxford: Blackwell, 1989), p. 160.

with immortality, and forgets to reckon with death".[5] Witnesses of this kind of anxiety which is interwoven with the drive to be unique, to be original come in the shape of influential books on literary theory such as Walter Jackson Bate's *The Burden of the Past* (1970), or Harold Bloom's *The Anxiety of Influence* (1972) and more recently Thomas McFarland's *Originality and Imagination* (1985).

They do, however, also contribute to our anxiety. All three participate in what could be tentatively described here as a "double-bind" where the fear of losing one's identity prevents the individual from finding it. To put it more provocatively, Bate's account of a tradition-weary poetic consciousness as well as Bloom's "intra-poetic" theory, and McFarland's ostensibly relational "originality paradox" subscribe in varying degrees to descriptions of our world raised to the status of universal frames of reference, that do not serve their function, but instead turn, as it were, against their makers.

Less involved and correspondingly more detached observations, however, evoke a different view of "originality". With the help of two strong voices of the past it could be expressed as a kind of "repetition"[6], of what otherwise would remain mere information, "historische Bildung".[7] Which, in a more contemporary language, is to say: a view of "originality" emerges that can be understood as a rediscription of the "literal", a rediscription of an inherited language into a "metaphor which we can find a use for".[8]

It is thus the recognition of a process that goes hand in hand with a more productive discussion of "originality". This in turn suggests a conception of human beings forming endless webs of interdependencies rather than splitting into isolated egos, into "we-less I's",[9] into the kind of closed personalities Elias refers to as "homo clausus".[10] Patterns of thought that suggest a rigid barrier between individuals are, however, deeply ingrained in our language. It is thus quite common to speak of the "individual" *and* "society". To this autonomist human self-image "Elias counterposes his own conceptual starting point of *homines aperti*

---

[5] Milan Kundera, *Immortality*, trans. Peter Kussi, (New York: Grove, 1990), p. 74.

[6] Søren Kierkegaard, "Repetition: a Venture in Experimenting Psychology by Constantin Constantius," in: *Kierkegaard's Writings*, vol. VI, (Princeton: Princeton University Press, 1983), p. 131: "Repetition and recollection are the same movement, except in opposite directions, or what is recollected forward. Repetition, therefore, if it is possible, makes a person happy, whereas recollection makes him unhappy."

[7] Friedrich Nietzsche, "Vom Nutzen und Nachteil der Historie für das Leben," in: *Werke*, vol. I, ed. Karl Schlechta, (Frankfurt/M: Ullstein, 1976), p. 209–285.

[8] Richard Rorty, *Contingency, irony and, solidarity*, (Cambridge: Cambridge University Press, 1989), p. 37.

[9] Cf. Norbert Elias, *Die Gesellschaft der Individuen*, ed. Michael Schröter, (Frankfurt/M: Suhrkamp, 1987), p. 13.

[10] Norbert Elias, *Was ist Soziologie?*, (Juventa: Weinheim, 1986), p. 128.

[...] bonded together in various ways and degrees".[11] This "figurational" human self-image in turn evokes a conception of "originality" which brings the continuous networks of human interdependencies to bear upon our existing symbolic means of orientation.[12]

Given that there are no absolute beginnings and ends, "repetition", reappropriation, recreation, rearrangement, levels of synthesis, in short: "gathered thinking" are to be seen as synonyms — not antonyms — of "originality". "But, because *we* begin and end, we insist [as Northrop Frye suggests in his *The Great Code*] that beginnings and endings must be much more deeply built into the reality of things than the universe around us suggests, and we shape our myths accordingly".[13] With this paper I hope to lessen the appeal of such myths without increasing suspicions of arguing for a kind of "Disneyland of innovation". First, I would like to look at what has been termed the "originality paradox".

W. Jackson Bate's book *The Burden of the Past and the English Poet* aims at illuminating driving forces of poetic consciousness — forces, T. S. Eliot, for example, sought to capture in the title of an essay as *Tradition and the Individual Talent*. Whereas Eliot comes to understand the relationship between tradition and individuality as an "interlacing"[14] locus of opportunity for the "finely perfected medium in which special, or very varied, feelings are at liberty to enter into new combinations",[15] Bate points towards a continuously deepening sense of crisis. It is, in his view, caused by an ever increasing flood of tradition — a tradition we are commonly educated to simultaneously hold in esteem and reject in order to

---

[11] Mennell, op. cit., p. 189.

[12] "An die Stelle des Bildes vom Menschen als einer 'geschlossenen Persönlichkeit' — trotz seiner etwas andern Bedeutung ist der Ausdruck bezeichnend — tritt dann das Bild des Menschen als einer 'offenen Persönlichkeit', die im Verhältnis zu andern Menschen einen höheren oder geringeren Grad von relativer Autonomie, aber niemals absolute und totale Autonomie besitzt, die in der Tat von Grund auf Zeit ihres Lebens auf andere Menschen ausgerichtet und angewiesen, von andern Menschen abhängig ist. Das Geflecht der Angewiesenheiten von Menschen aufeinander, ihre Interdependenzen, sind das, was sie aneinander bindet. Sie sind das Kernstück dessen, was hier als Figuration bezeichnet wird, als Figuration aufeinander ausgerichteter, voneinander abhängiger Menschen." Norbert Elias, *Über den Prozeß der Zivilisation: soziogenetische und psychogenetische Untersuchungen. Erster Band*, (Frankfurt/M: Suhrkamp, 1976), p. LXVII.

[13] Northrop Frye, *The Great Code: the Bible and Literature*, (Toronto: Academic Press, 1982), p. 108.

[14] "Interlacing" [...] can be regarded either as a dramatist's defense against precursors (and contemporary rivals) or as the same dramatist's joyous disregard of the literary force of the past." Harold Bloom, *Modern Critical Views: Tom Stoppard*, (New York: Chelsea House, 1986), p. 1.

[15] T.S. Eliot, "Tradition and the Individual Talent," in: *Selected Prose of T.S. Eliot*, ed. Frank Kermode, (New York: Harcourt, 1975), p. 41.

assert our individuality.¹⁶ The answers Bate provides are guided by the thought of the past as a burden for the creative mind and thus necessarily remain variations of one question permeating his book: What in the face of past accomplishments *"is there left to do"* for the artist?¹⁷ How "to use a heritage, when we know and admire so much about it, how to grow by means of it, how to acquire our own 'identities,' how to be ourselves?"¹⁸

The observation of a perceived tension between tradition and individuality made by Bate and the insight that it cannot be resolved (as argued by Rorty) are merged by McFarland forging the paradigm for his book *Originality and Imagination*. Such a synthesis allows McFarland to make explicit the rhetorical nature of Bate's questions or, to put it differently, to describe the crisis-evoking relationship of the individual to his/her heritage in terms of a "fundamental" — albeit dynamic and correlative — opposition.¹⁹

> [It] must be realized [McFarland argues] that this crisis consists of an intensification of elements permanently present, and not the historical appearance of new reality. To realize this is to grasp a major significance of the originality paradox. The paradox is in fact a paradox, and not a merely historical development,²⁰

---

[16] "It is built into the basic structure of the language [the child] is learning. It is rubbed in repeatedly with such remarks as, 'It isn't like you to do a thing like that.' Or, 'Don't be a copy-cat; be yourself!' Or, when one child imitates the mannerisms of another child whom he admires, 'Johnny, that's not you. That's Peter!' The innocent victim of this indoctrination cannot understand the paradox. He is being told that he *must* be free. An irresistable pressure is being put on him to make him believe that no such pressure exists. The community of which he is necessarily a dependent member defines him as an independent member." Alan Watts, *The Book: On the Taboo Against Knowing Who You Are*, (New York: Vintage, 1972), p. 65 f.

[17] W. Jackson Bate, *The Burden of the Past and the English Poet*, (Cambridge: Harvard University Press, 1979), p. 3.

[18] Ibidem, p. 134.

[19] In McFarland's review of Bloom's *Anxiety of Influence* the here hidden egocentrism finds much more open expression. He, for example, criticizes that Bloom "too radically dissipates what the common voice of humanity has always intuitively [!] identified as the special truth about the lyric poet: his [!] personal vision." When McFarland argues that Bloom's treatment of Wallace Stevens is onesided since "he goes too far in refusing to allow any credence at all to Stevens' considered testimony of personal originality" he supports his criticism of Bloom with a statement which mirrors the influence of the geocentric world view on his own thinking perhaps most markedly: "Each of us is," McFarland claims, "the isolated ego of d'Alembert's dream, occupying the center of a uniquely personal web of sensations and experiences." *Commonweal*, (November 2, 1973), p. 113.

[20] Most present-day research is conducted with the goal to disclose immutable patterns and abstract them from diachronic change, which is usually devalued as the 'merely historical'." Norbert Elias, *Involvement and Detachment*, trans. Edmund Jephcott, (Oxford: Blackwell, 1987), p. 125.

simply because it is always present and defies resolution.[21]

For McFarland there seems to be no doubt that "the full truth is a tension of opposites. There is tradition, and tradition is extraordinarily important; but there is also such a reality as individual talent."[22]

How, indeed, could it be otherwise? For McFarland carries his thesis to the very boundaries of his frame of reference. However, he argues from within these boundaries *without* recognizing them, as if they had disappeared, as if there were no worlds beyond — hence the sense of closure evoked by his 'atomistic' language. To put it differently, he is involved in this language to a degree that the imagined destination reached in his quest for more detached evaluations is to be "real" and "final" — or, in McFarland's own words, "the full truth."[23]

Myths of departure as well as myths of arrival make it more difficult for us to see that there are no beginnings, no ends — except those created by an imagination that asks questions shaped by a "deepseated nostalgia for the absolute" which, as Steiner claims, prevail in our culture, our political orders, our metaphysical notions.[24]

> Like never before, today at this point in the twentieth century, we hunger for myths, for total explanation: we are starving for guaranteed prophecy.[25]

"We naturally want (desire as well as lack)," Douglas Atkins writes in 1983, "the comfort and solace afforded by a (fantasized) world in which conclusions are possible."[26] Truth, in the words of Mario Vargas Llosa, "is in the mind, in imagination and reason — not hidden like a treasure in the depths of matter or in the stellar abyss."[27]

Seen, therefore, from a more detached point of view, such as Llosa's, the "limiting," the "de-finition" (*definitio*; lat. for a limiting, prescribing) of "originality", or the relationship between individual and tradition, offered by McFarland can be thought of as an illustration of the illusionary quality of any teleologically

---

[21] Thomas McFarland, *Originality and Imagination*, (Baltimore: Johns Hopkins University Press, 1985), p. 14.

[22] Ibidem, p. 58. Other such examples include: "[...] the tension between the individual and society [...]" (p. 3); "That the conception of 'Originals' existed in polar tension to the conception of tradition and thereby participated fully in the originality paradox was central to Young's existence." (p. 6); "[...] Eliot reasserts the dynamic interplay of the two realities." (p. 10); "That paradox is a constant of all culture that is not preliterate [...] it cannot be resolved." (p. 22).

[23] Ibidem, p. 58.

[24] George Steiner, *Nostalgia for the Absolute*, (Toronto: CBC Publications, 1974), p. 5.

[25] Ibidem, p. 5 f.

[26] G. Douglas Atkins, *Reading Deconstruction Deconstructive Reading*, ([Lexington]: University Press of Kentucky, 1983), p. 136.

[27] Mario Vargas Llosa, "Updating Karl Popper", *PMLA* 105.5 (October, 1990), p. 1018.

inspired re-presentation where epistemological refinements appear in the disguise of ontological absolutes. To put the same point in another way, the meaning of "originality" is contingent upon the method employed; it depends on what the respective frame of reference allows "originality" to mean, it depends on the circle within which the quadrature of "originality" is to take place. "A map *is* [after all] *not*", as Alfred Korzybski pointed out in 1933, "the territory it represents [...]. If the map could be ideally correct, it would include, in a reduced scale, the map of the map; the map of the map, of the map; and so on, endlessly."[28] One explanation for this claim is well known: the map cannot be the territory because re-presentations are subject to the mimetic limitations of language. If this is to say that only a super-language, a language out of reach for human beings, would enable us to capture the territory as it *truly is* — rather than as it *truly is becoming* — then we may have created another obstacle for a more useful "truth": It would be more difficult for us to see that "territory" refers to something quite other than the expression *terra firma*, the solid ground within a well defined area, suggests: namely human figurations in the civilizing process — "networks of interdependent human beings, with shifting asymmetrical power balances."[29]

Thus, the truth claim made by McFarland with respect to his originality paradox is more adequately described as "simply a compliment paid to sentences seen to be paying their way."[30] The originality paradox reflects human-made truths which resulted from a particular human-made method. Or, to be more precise and to correct the impression of subscribing to some kind of collective voluntarism: "The method which people use in acquiring knowledge is functionally interdependent with, and thus inseparable from, the substance of the knowledge they possess, and especially from their basic image of the world."[31]

In itself it is not a difficulty, it is simply a necessity that "truths" — as firmly rooted in our habits of thought as they commonly are — are of our own making. The difficulty instead arises where methods, descriptions of our world raised to the status of a universal frame of reference, do not serve their function, where, indeed, methods turn, as it were, against their makers, where resulting truths are *not* "paying their way."[32] And this, I would like to argue with reference to Norbert Elias, is the case with presuppositions such as the one underlying the

---

[28] Alfred Korzybski, *Science and Sanity: An Introduction to Non-Aristotelian Systems and General Semantics*, (Lakeville: Non-Aristotelian Library, 1973), p. 58.

[29] See Mennell, op. cit., p. 252.

[30] See Bernard Williams, "Auto-da-Fé: Consequences of Pragmatism," in: *Reading Rorty*, ed. Alan Malachowski, (Oxford; Blackwell, 1990), p. 30.

[31] Elias, *Involvement*, op. cit., p. 64.

[32] "Truth is, in the first instance, a hypothesis or a theory that attempts to solve a problem." Llosa, op. cit., p. 1018.

thesis of McFarland's originality paradox:

> There is no end to it, nothing can ever reconcile the polar views and solve the problems arising from the fictitious assumption of an existential gulf between human beings and the world they set out to discover and to control — the world of which they themselves form part. This assumption is the stumbling block. Nothing new, no advances in the theory of knowledge and of sciences are possible as long as the assumptions of an ontological gulf between "subject" and "object", explicitly or not, remains the basis of these theories.[33]

To reason more specifically that a frame of reference based on a presupposed absolute break between tradition and individuality is not only blocking advances in the theory of knowledge but indeed bound to debilitate, one could begin by referring to Roland Barthes. This would help us here to point more directly to the vulnerability of the assumptions underlying the observations made by Bate and McFarland: we could indicate that these assumptions strongly subscribe to a hierarchical view of values which attribute foremost epistemic relevance to human-made "truths" such as "first principles", "priority", "origin", "essence" etc. "We know now," Barthes insists in his essay *The death of the author*, "that a text is not a line of words releasing a single 'theological' meaning [...] but a multidimensional space in which a variety of writings, none of them original, blend and clash."[34] As "today emerges from yesterday"[35] texts for Barthes thus take the shape of a "tissue of quotations drawn from the innumerable centres of culture."[36]

Harold Bloom's *Anxiety of Influence* profits from these insights and is thus able to offer a most inclusive discussion of the relationship between tradition and individuality. His book, to be sure, centers around the questions posed by Bate. "Everything that makes up this book", Bloom comments, "intends to be part of a unified meditation on the melancholy of the creative mind's desperate insistence upon priority."[37] The relative sameness of the terrain both set out to map is perhaps most obvious in instances such as the following:

> How can they [poets] give pleasure, if in no way they have received it? But how can they receive the deepest pleasure, the ecstasy of priority, of self-begetting, of

---

[33] Norbert Elias, "Scientific Establishments," in: *Scientific Establishments and Hierarchies*, ed. N. Elias, R. Whitley, H.G. Martins, (Dordrecht: Reidel, 1982), p. 23 f.

[34] Roland Barthes, "The death of the author," in: *Modern Criticism and Theory*, ed. David Lodge, (London: Longman, 1988), p. 170.

[35] Roland Barthes, *The Pleasure of the Text*, trans. Richard Miller, (New York: Noonday Press, 1988), p. 20.

[36] Barthes, "death of the author", op. cit., p. 170.

[37] Harold Bloom, *The Anxiety of Influence: A Theory of Poetry*, (Oxford: Oxford University Press, 1975), p. 13.

an assured autonomy, if their way to the True Subject and their own True Selves lies through the precursor's subject and his self? [38]

Bloom, however, shares in the discours exemplified here by instances of Barthes' thought. He for example argues that we "need to stop thinking of any poet as an autonomous ego, however solipsistic the strongest of poets may be. Every poet is a being caught up in a dialectical relationship [...] with another poet or poets."[39] The prominent line of his theory of poetry, "[t]he meaning of a poem can only be another poem" conveys this "intertextual" mode of perception in perhaps the most memorable way.[40] Bloom, in other words, reaches a perspective which allows him to move beyond a 'fuller', more refined description of Bate's accomplishments. He is in a position to write from a more inclusive, not additive and indifferent but "gathered" and thus more detached point of view than his immediate predecessor(s) and, for that matter, McFarland indicate.[41] The perspective that emerges for Bloom (according to this reading of Bloom) I will refer to in the subsequent synthesis as "originality 'double-bind'."

The term "double-bind" suggests a circular, reciprocal (and potentially self-escalating) process where a high degree of danger and its pendant, a correspondingly high degree of emotive involvement continously reproduce each other. In *Involvement and Detachment* (1983) Norbert Elias argues:

> If the danger which one group of humans represents for another is high, the emotivity of thinking, its fantasy-content, is also likely to remain high. If the fantasy-content of thinking and knowledge is high and thus its reality-orientation low, the ability of both sides to bring the situation under control will also remain low, the danger level and the level of fear will remain high, and so on *ad infinitum*.[42]

In this light, we can think of *Anxiety of Influence* in terms of descriptions of poetic consciousness from three vantage points — each located on a continuum of "involvement" and "detachment": 1) a description of poetic consciousness from the poets' vantage point, 2) a description of poetic consciousness from Bloom's vantage point, and 3) a description of poetic consciousness from this reader's vantage point.

The perception of the poets is seen as a linear progression ranging from an

---

[38] Ibidem, p. 116. "It seems almost," Alan Watts wrote in 1966, "as if to be is to quarrel, or at least to differ, to be in contrast with something else. If so, whoever does not put up a fight has no identity; whoever is not self-ish has no identity." Op. cit., p. 109 f.

[39] Bloom, *Anxiety*, op. cit., p. 91.

[40] Ibidem, p. 94.

[41] McFarland's *Originality and Imagination* was published 1985, 13 years after Bloom's *Anxiety of Influence*.

[42] Op. cit., p. 99.

anxiety ridden awareness of tradition to the presumambly liberating status of a poet in his/her own right: We begin with a poetic consciousness highly aware of a growing tradition and deeply affected by an anxiety of drowning in this tradition. The poet seeks to escape the perceived threat. His/her desire is thus aimed at achieving a distinct position as poet separating him/her from tradition. The fulfilment of this desire, the successful escape from tradition has been variously labeled as, for example, "marginal differentiation", "truth", "privileged language", "self-creation" but perhaps most commonly as "originality".

A more detached view, a view "not participating in the high value of the discovery of eternals" presumably open to Bloom's but not to the poets' consciousness reveals a circular movement, a double-bind:[43] The thought of being in danger (of drowning in tradition) is contingent upon the possibility of "originality", of a self separated from tradition. Thinking of having escaped drowning in tradition by asserting the self through "originality" thus becomes a function of the danger itself. The perceived danger in turn invokes the ostensible escape through "originality". To desire "originality" is thus to desire the anxiety of influence.

The functional interdependence between our desire to assert a self and the degree of anxiety experienced, is, in more general terms, perhaps best expressed as the double-bind of "process-control" (here: danger of drowning in tradition) and "self-control" (here: need to assert the self through "originality"). A low ability to control the impression of drowning in tradition thus can be thought of as going hand in hand with a low ability to control the need to assert a self.[44]

To summarize: Collective fantasies, fictions of the self as, for example "originality", impede a more detached, albeit emotionally less appealing, view thus feeding anxieties of drowning in tradition not allowing to achieve any measure of control over our anxieties other than the mere illusion of having done so.

Not only, however, are these "solutions" illusory but they are principal participants in the originality double-bind. It is as if those poets are like the transcendental philosophers Elias describes whose fear of losing their identity prevents them from finding it:

> There is an obvious way of escape from the impass where, for centuries, transcendental philosophers have found themselves trapped. That way, however, is closed to them. They cannot use it without loosing their identity.[45]

The third vantage point, also located on a continuum — consisting of compounds of "involvement" and "detachment" — , that of the reader of Bloom's *Anxiety of Influence*, I would like to approach with the help of McFarland's and Bloom's reading of Goethe.

---

[43] Elias, "Scientific Establishments," op. cit., p. 32.

[44] See Elias, *Involvement*, op. cit., p. 45–118.

[45] "Scientific Establishments," op. cit., p. 15.

The following passage from Goethe's conversations with Eckermann was chosen by Bloom as well as McFarland in support of their respective arguments:

> Man spricht immer von Originalität, allein was will das sagen! Sowie wir geboren werden, fängt die Welt an, auf uns zu wirken, und das geht so fort bis ans Ende. Und überall! was können wir denn unser Eigenes nennen, als die Energie, die Kraft, das Wollen![46]

In discussing the term 'plagiarism' McFarland reaches the conclusion that it is not a category distinguishable in kind from "originality." Plagiarism, in McFarland's opinion, has to be seen in the context of the originality paradox: Plagiarism, McFarland claims, "is a practice that participates in and is witness to the paradox that surrounds the entire conception of originality."[47] Goethe's insistence upon being indebted to his predecessors with the exception of the energy, the strength, and the will, is cited by McFarland as part of the discussion on plagiarism and characterized as "what must be the eternal limit on the claims for" the conception of "originality."[48] However, the word "eternal" betrays the limits of McFarland's argument. It is as if one were asked not to question anymore and to suspend any argument that might point to a different reading of Goethe.

Whereas McFarland may have mistaken everlasting limits of his frame of reference for those of Goethe, Bloom feels compelled to categorize Goethe as one of the "great deniers of influence,"[49] "miraculously free of" the anxiety of influence.[50] Bloom reads passages of Goethe selected by him as an implicit claim to that which is outside the humanly possible, to that which is divine.[51] Since "self-appropriation," so Bloom, "involves the immense anxieties of indebtedness"[52] Goethe's position is seen as a sign of no less than "appalling self-confidence."[53]

And what about Bloom's self-confidence? Bloom's own need to assert his self as critic, I would like to suggest, prevents him from reaching an even more detached view than his assessment of poetic consciousness displays. As a matter of fact, a reader of Bloom's *Anxiety of Influence* might even reverse the argument put forth by Bloom: It is Bloom — not Goethe — who lays claim to the privileged

---

[46] Johann Wolfgang Goethe, *Gedenkausgabe der Werke, Briefe und Gespräche*, vol. XXIV, ed. Ernst Beutler, (Zürich: Artemis, 1976), p. 158 f.

[47] Op. cit., p. 29.

[48] Ibidem, p. 29.

[49] *Anxiety*, op. cit., p. 56.

[50] Ibidem, p. 60.

[51] Ibidem, p. 52.

[52] Ibidem, p. 5.

[53] Ibidem, p. 52.

position attributed to Goethe. In order to escape the "horror", to use Bloom's words, "of finding himself to be only a copy or a replica" it has become necessary, as it were, to misread Goethe.[54] Goethe thus cannot share in Bloom's "discovery" of the double-bind of the anxiety ridden desire for that "minimal and figurative immortality" and the ficticiousness of any claim to constitute an origin.[55] Isn't Bloom thus offering a reading of his reading of Goethe when he reiterates the main argument of *Anxiety of Influence* in his *map of misreading* (1975)? "An intolerable presence (the precursor's poem) has been voided, and the new poem starts in the *illusio* that this absence can deceive us into accepting a new presence."[56]

Is Bloom, in other words, guilty of the very same separation of tradition and individuality he himself helped to identify as an illusion charateristic of poetic consciousness? Such an assessment would belie his achievment. It would blur the difference between his assessment of poetic consciousness (which points towards a separation of tradition and individuality) and the position Bloom himself displays through his assessment. We therefore need to avoid reading Bloom "in terms of a static polarity between total 'objectivity' and total 'subjectivity'"[57] since it is "a matter not of polar contrasts but of a continuum along which blends of 'involvement' and 'detachment' are located."[58] Bloom, one could argue with the help of this model, participates in a double-bind displaying a high degree of detachment and a degree of involvement which does not yet allow him to control his need to assert his self to a point where he could reach an even more detached perspective. A perspective which would allow him to say that his insight does not correspond to a beginning, an origin in our knowledge that coincides with his person but a relatively detached perspective which is in principal open to all, including the poetic consciousness of Goethe.

In the case of Goethe, there is evidence, such as his criticism of Plato and Descartes, which points in the direction of a figurational rather than egocentric human self-image:

> Er [Plato] dringt in die Tiefen, mehr um sie mit seinem Wesen auszufüllen, als um sie zu erforschen. Er bewegt sich nach der Höhe, mit Sehnsucht, seines Ursprungs wieder teilhaft zu werden. Alles, was er äußert, bezieht sich auf ein ewig Ganzes, Gutes, Wahres, Schönes, dessen Forderung er in jedem Busen aufzuregen strebt.[59]

---

[54] Ibidem, p. 80.

[55] Ibidem, p. 149.

[56] Harold Bloom, *A map of misreading*, (New York: Oxford University Press, 1975), p. 71.

[57] Mennell, op. cit., p. 160.

[58] Ibidem, p. 160.

[59] Op. cit., vol. XVI, p. 346.

Goethe's discussion of Descartes reveals his relational understanding of the word "originality" with particular force:

> Cartesius' Verdienste um den Regenbogen sind nicht zu leugnen. Aber auch hier, wie in andern Fällen, ist er gegen seine Vorgänger nicht dankbar. Er will nun ein für allemal ganz original sein; er lehnt nicht allein die lästige Autorität ab, sondern auch die förderliche.[60]

Predecessors whose work will be part of another, more inclusive synthesis are thus seen by Goethe as benefactors rather than rivals. On the topic of "plagiarism" Goethe wrote:

> Dagegen müssen wir den bildenden Künstler in Schutz nehmen, welcher nicht verdient Plagiarier genannt zu werden, wenn er schon vorhandene, gebrauchte, ja bis auf einen gewissen Grad gesteigerte Motive nochmals behandelt. Die Menge, die einen falschen Begriff von Originalität hat, glaubt ihn deshalb tadeln zu dürfen, anstatt daß er höchlich zu loben ist, wenn er irgend etwas schon Vorhandenes auf einen höhern, ja den höchsten Grad der Bearbeitung bringt. Nicht allein den Stoff empfangen wir von außen, auch fremden Gehalt dürfen wir uns aneignen, wenn nur eine gesteigerte, wo nicht vollendete Form uns angehört. Ebenso kann und muß auch der Gelehrte seine Vorgänger benutzen, ohne jedesmal ängstlich anzudeuten, woher es ihm gekommen; versäumen wird er aber niemals, seine Dankbarkeit gelegentlich auszudrücken gegen die Wohltäter, welche die Welt ihm aufgeschlossen; es mag nun sein, daß er ihnen Ansicht über das Ganze oder Einsicht ins Einzelne verdankt.[61]

In more general terms, the question thus arises whether this particular, or for that matter any blend of involvement and detachment can still adequately be described solely in terms of "anxiety". Are we, to put it with the help of Ryszard Kapuscinski's description of emperor Haile Selassie, still subject to a degree of involvement which compels us to believe that there "can be only one sun [since such] is the order of nature, and anything else is heresy?"[62] Postmodernist responses, which argue for "truth" in the plural,[63] for "truth" as a means to an end, for a "return

---

[60] Ibidem, p. 440.

[61] Ibidem, p. 915. Other "hard evidence" includes statements by Goethe such as: "Der törigste von allen Irrtümern ist, wenn junge gute Köpfe glauben, ihre Originalität zu verlieren, indem sie das Wahre anerkennen, was von andern schon anerkannt worden." Ibidem, vol. IX, p. 524.

"Ist er [der zur Vernunft geborene Mensch] nun nicht geneigt, von höher ausgebildeten Künstlern der Vor- und Mitzeit das zu lernen, was ihm fehlt, um eigentlicher Künstler zu sein, so wird er im falschen Begriff von bewahrter Originalität hinter sich selbst zurückbleiben; denn nicht allein das, was mit uns geboren ist, sondern auch das, was wir erwerben können, gehört uns an und wir sind es." Ibidem, vol. IX, p. 558.

[62] Ryszard Kapuscinski, *The Emperor*, (London: Picador, 1984), p. 33.

[63] Rorty, op. cit,. p. 21.

of the Many"⁶⁴ are widely accepted contemporary correctives aginst our present desire for "'sacred' truths".⁶⁵ They bear witness to a level of detachment which is more inclusive and thus less "totalistic", less "totalitarian", and thus in turn less anxiety ridden.⁶⁶

This is not to say that it would be more productive to simply substitute pleasure for anxiety. A kind of "erotics" of innovation, to borrow from Susan Sontag's *Against interpretation*,⁶⁷ would be the consequence of this point of departure which subscribes to what more recently has been labeled "radical indeterminacy".⁶⁸ In the case of Goethe, this "monism of absence", as Calinescu put it, would mean turning a blind eye towards readings pointing to his involvement, his egocentrism, his desire to be unique.⁶⁹ In the more vivid words of Milan Kundera's latest novel *Immortality*, we would fail to see the Goethe who "had been so careful not to depart for immortality with a rumpled shirt."⁷⁰

Given the means of orientation available to us in the shape of the figurationaly inspired conception of involvement and detachment one could say in conclusion: "originality" cannot be adequately discussed *either* in terms of dichotomies such as "subject" vs. "object" *or* in terms of an "endless textuality."⁷¹ It indeed seems more productive to speak of "originality" in terms of balances of anxiety *and* pleasure.

The limitations of Bloom and McFarland we identified with the help of their respective readings of Goethe are thus not so much the result of two untenable claims to privileged insight (in McFarland's case the originality-paradox, in Bloom's case the originality double-bind) but rather a question of particular blends of involvement and detachment — blends which signify balances of anxiety *and* pleasure.

---

⁶⁴ Matei Calinescu, "From the One to the Many: Pluralism in Today's Thought," in: *Innovation/Renovation: New Perspectives on the Humanities*, ed. Ihab Hassan and Sally Hassan, (Madison: University of Wisconsin Press, 1983), p. 264.

⁶⁵ Llosa, op. cit., p. 1019.

⁶⁶ See Calinescu, op. cit., p. 268 f.

⁶⁷ Susan Sontag, *Against interpretation and Other Essays*, (New York: Octagon Books, 1982), p. 14.

⁶⁸ Hans Bertens, "The Postmodern Weltanschauung and its Relation with Modernism: An Introductory Survey," in: *Approaching Postmodernism*, ed. Douwe Fokkema and Hans Bertens, (Amsterdam: John Benjamins, 1986), p. 45.

⁶⁹ Op. cit., p. 272.

⁷⁰ Kundera, op. cit., p. 70.

⁷¹ Andreas Huyssen, *After the Great Divide: Modernism, Mass Culture, Postmodernism*, (Bloomington: University of Indiana Press, 1986), p. 182.

Priscilla Hayden-Roy

Sensate Language and the Hermetic Tradition in Friedrich Christoph Oetinger's *Biblisches und Emblematisches Wörterbuch*

THE RISE OF RATIONALISTIC MORAL theology in the 18th century reflects the prevailing assumption of Enlightened thought that moral concepts were the privileged hermeneutical telos of the "coarse" or sensate language in the Bible and Christian dogma. The theological school known as neology supported this view and proposed an exegetical strategy for extracting the "pure" moral sense from the "coarse" or sensate text. In 1772 the Berlin neologian Wilhelm Abraham Teller (1734-1804) published a programmatic guide to this exegetical strategy, a dictionary entitled *Wörterbuch des Neuen Testaments zur Erklärung der christlichen Lehre*.[1]

I would like to discuss here a critical response to Teller's dictionary, written by the Württemberg pietist, Friedrich Christoph Oetinger (1702-1782). Oetinger, a member of the clergy in Lutheran Württemberg, was a leader of the speculative wing of Württemberg pietists who were influenced by Jacob Böhme, the cabala, alchemy, and even Swedenborg.[2] In the following I will discuss the background and implications of Oetinger's notion of sensate language, its connection to hermetic and theosophical traditions of the 18th century, and its polemical function as an alternative to the rational discourse of moral philosophy. I will then draw some parallels to developments in late 18th-century aesthetic philosophy.

Oetinger's theology directs a polemic against all "idealist" privileging of spirit over body,[3] particularly the philosophies of Leibniz and Wolff. Originally a

---

[1] Citations are from the 5th edition (1792); references to this edition hereafter as *WB*.

[2] Oetinger published the first German translation of Swedenborg's works: *Swedenborgs und anderer irrdische und himmlische Philosophie* ... , 2 vols. (Frankfurt, Leipzig: Garbe, 1765).

[3] "Daß das Fleisch in ein ewiges Leben versezt werden kan, und doch körperlich bleibt, daß die Fülle der Gottheit in Christo körperlich werden kan, und daß der Geist zu einem Körper werden kan, ist auch daraus klar, wiewol es den Idealistischen Wissern nicht in Kopf will. Plato hat den Grund zu dem Idealismo gelegt, indem er vorgegeben: was körperlich seye, habe kein wahres Wesen." Friedrich Christoph Oetinger, *Biblisches und Emblematisches Wörterbuch* (1776; Hildesheim: Georg Olms, 1969) 100. References to this work hereafter as *BEW*.

disciple of these men, he was led to his anti-idealist position as a student, through his extra-curricular reading of Jacob Böhme, whose works the powder miller in Tübingen urged him to read. His convictions were strengthened through extensive study of alchemy and the cabala — the latter study undertaken under the tutelage of Jewish rabbis in Frankfurt and Halle.[4] At the center of Oetinger's thought is a dynamic notion of God's progressive self-corporealization in creation and history, which occurs through the interaction of mutually opposing, life-generating forces — the ten sephirot in the cabala.[5] These forces within nature drive all things toward their perfect end, "Geistleiblichkeit," or flesh imbued with spirit. Oetinger incorporates this theosophical process within the framework of Christian salvation history. He conceives of the fall as a disruption of the originally harmonious interaction of divine forces, whereby individual forces are unleashed from their submission to the whole, setting flesh in opposition to spirit. Christ, conceived in cabalistic terms as the "Zaemach,"[6] or lively substance within all things, initiates the restoration of original harmony through his death and

---

[4] Oetinger relates his intellectual development in his autobiography, printed in *Friedrich Christoph Oetingers Leben und Briefe, als urkundlicher Commentar zu dessen Schriften*, ed. Karl Chr. Eberh. Ehmann (Stuttgart: F.J. Steinkopf, 1859). See also Martin Weyer-Menkhoff, *Christus, das Heil der Natur: Entstehung und Systematik der Theologie Friedrich Christoph Oetingers*, Arbeiten zur Geschichte des Pietismus, Vol. 27 (Göttingen: Vandenhoeck & Ruprecht, 1990).

[5] Oetinger modifies the cabalistic ten sephirot by identifying the first three with the trinity and ascribing to them a special status restricted to the godhead, while the latter seven emanate into creation. Thus Oetinger most commonly refers only to the "seven spirits," as they are the vehicle of God's corporealization in creation. Sigrid Großmann has noted that Oetinger vacillates in his explication of the trinity, at times employing cabalistic terminology which equates the parts of the trinity with forces or principles, at other times espousing the orthodox teaching of the three persons of the trinity. (*Friedrich Christoph Oetingers Gottesvorstellung: Versuch einer Analyse seiner Theologie*, Arbeiten zur Geschichte des Pietismus, Vol. 18 [Göttingen: Vandenhoeck & Ruprecht, 1979] 277 ff.)

[6] Oetinger draws the expression from Zecharia 3:8, 6:12; it is a messianic title meaning "branch" or "shoot." The conception of Christ as "Zaemach," or an organic, enlivening principle, is the point of contact to many other sources Oetinger eclectically appropriates. Notably he interprets Paul in this light: "Paulo beliebt, nach creatürlichen Art, unter dem Bild des säens und erndtens, vom Geist zu reden, weil der Geist in Wahrheit ein vegetabilisch Gewächs und ein Baum des Lebens ist [...]. Siehe, mein Knecht heißt Zaemach, 'das gewächsliche Leben'; unter ihm wird es wachsen (Zach. 6[,12]). Geist ist also die gantze gewächsliche Verfassung des treibenden Göttlichen Lebens" (*Die Lehrtafel der Prinzessin Antonia*, ed. Reinhard Breymayer, Friedrich Häussermann, 2 vols. [Berlin, NY: Walter de Gruyter, 1977] 1: 193). The Böhmian and alchemical concept of "tincture" is also seen in connection with "Zaemach": "Folglich ist die Tinctur das Haupt-Instrument alles Wachsens, davon JEsus Zaemach heißt, denn unter ihm wird alles wachsen" (*BEW* 622). Oetinger draws on the French medic Claude-Nicolas LeCat's (1700-1768) notion of a "fluide des nerfs" in discussing the presence of this tincture, or lively substance, within living organisms (*Lehrtafel* 1: 100; *BEW* 620). With all these concepts Oetinger's purpose is to designate a substance or principle capable of mediating between the spiritual and material realms, so that he can explain that concept most central to his theology, *Geistleiblichkeit*.

resurrection. His blood, possessing the transmuting power of an alchemical "tincture,"[7] begins the revivifying process by being poured out on the earth. His resurrected body is the guarantor of the restoration of harmony in all creation, when, in Pauline terms, Christ becomes "all in all,"[8] that is, when the glory of God is manifested fully in corporeal form.

Oetinger's biblical hermeneutics applies this same principle of corporealization to the text. The words of Scripture yield meaning in the same manner that spirit emanates into bodies: their fundamental structure is a "generative order" that unfolds as the plant from a seed. The image of the seed suggests both semantic plenitude and nexus within plenitude: Oetinger calls the words of Scripture "pregnant,"[9] ramifying outward into a vast nexus of sensate meaning. This contrasts with the exegetical approach of those theologians influenced by rationalism, who project onto Scripture a "geometrical order," as Oetinger calls it, whereby an abstract concept constitutes the hermeneutical center of the Bible.[10] These exegetes, argues Oetinger, "peel off" ("abschelen") the pregnant, sensate meaning of Scripture. By reducing the words to abstract concepts they make Scripture "overly distinct" ("überdeutlich"), and ultimately construct an arbitrary or idiosyncratic system of doctrine that fails to grasp the whole of

---

[7] "Die Tinctur des Bluts Christi wird uns die Gestalten der Dinge im Geist darstellen. Es wird wirklich gesprengt, wie seine Bluts-Tropfen auf die Erden gefallen, und schon einen Theil des Fluchs hinweg nahmen." (*BEW* 80).

[8] The phrase "Alles in Allem" (τὰ πάντα ἐν πᾶσιν), found in numerous places in the Pauline epistles (I Cor. 15:28, Eph. 1:23, Col. 3:11) was a favorite among the speculative pietists in Württemberg and was usually found in tandem with the heterodox teaching of the "Wiederbringung aller Dinge" (ἀποκατάστασις πάντων), to which Oetinger also subscribed. See Friedhelm Groth, *Die "Wiederbringung aller Dinge" im württembergischen Pietismus. Theologiegeschichtliche Studien zum eschatologischen Heilsuniversalismus württembergischer Pietisten des 18. Jahrhunderts*, Arbeiten zur Geschichte des Pietismus, Vol. 21 (Göttingen: Vandenhoeck & Ruprecht, 1984).

[9] "Die Worte der Schrift sind prägnant, d.i. vielbegreifende Worte, wie die Ebräische Sprache." (*BEW* 285)

[10] "Die heil[ige]. Schrift bedient sich einer Methode, welche mehr mit der Entstehung der Dinge übereinkommt und nicht so gar sehr auf die Concinnitat der Begriffe ausgeht. Die geometrische Ordnung nimmt ihren Ausgangspunkt von irgend einem abstrakten Gedanken, die generative Ordnung aber geht, wie es beim Samenkorn der Fall ist, vom Ganzen aus, und entfaltet dieses gleichmäßig bis zum Kleinsten." Friedrich Christoph Oetinger, *Die Theologie aus der Idee des Lebens abgeleitet und auf sechs Stücke zurückgeführt, deren jedes nach dem sensus communis, dann nach den Geheimnissen der Schrift, endlich nach dogmatischen Formeln, auf eine neue und erfahrungsmäßige Weise abgehandelt wird*, tr. Julius Hamberger (Stuttgart: J. F. Steinkopf, 1852), 35.

truth.[11] We can see here a clear inversion of valuation as Oetinger marks that goal of Wolffian hermeneutics — distinctness — with a negative valence.

Oetinger found a prime example of the "overly distinct" exegesis of the "geometrical order" in Teller's *Wörterbuch*. In 1776, four years after Teller's dictionary appeared, Oetinger published his anonymous[12] response, the *Biblisches und Emblematisches Wörterbuch*. In his foreword he writes that the assumption of Teller and other theologians that the sensate language in Scripture was mere "Jewish word games" is the chief error of his day.[13] Biblical language is sensual and "massive" by intention, argues Oetinger: "die Sinnlichkeit der Schrift [ist] die Hauptabsicht GOttes" (*BEW*, Vorrede [6v]). Teller's "disrobing" attenuates and distorts meaning,[14] says Oetinger, for spirit is not an abstraction or naked moral truth, but rather an "enveloped" vital principle whose meaning consists in the unfolding ("Auswicklung") of the seed-like, dynamically ramifying spirit.[15] For this reason the Bible's fundamental concepts are not to be understood with precise, univocal definitions, argues Oetinger, but by viewing the plenitude of sensate images or emblems ("Sinnbilder") employed in the Bible to illustrate the concept. On the concept of righteousness, for example, Oetinger writes:

> Gerechtigkeit wird in heiliger Schrift nie mit Definitionen erklärt, wie sich überhaupt die Schrift wenig bedient, sondern durch alle Sinnbilder der Natur, und durch unzählige Beziehungen Subjectorum und Praedicatorum erläutert (*BEW* 260).

---

[11] "Wer nun auf geometrische Art mit den Worten der Schrift umgehet, da man einen gewissen Theil dieses prägnanten Sinns abschelet, in gewisse Ueberdeutlichkeit stellt, und daraus ein ganzes System von Lehr-Säzen durch rechte Schlüsse heraus spinnt, der hat den rechten Griff sich selbst eigensinnig zu machen gegen der ganzen Warheit" (*BEW* 285).

[12] Due to sharply critical reviews outside Württemberg of the Swedenborg book, the Württemberg Consistory curtailed Oetinger's publishing activity by requiring that he submit all his works to the Consistorial censure. Oetinger continued publishing, however: friends and relatives agreed to have the works published in their names outside Württemberg, or he had them published anonymously. See Gunther Franz, "Bücherzensur und Irenik," *Theologen und Theologie an der Universität Tübingen: Beiträge zur Geschichte der Evangelisch-Theologischen Fakultät*, ed. Martin Brecht (Tübingen: Mohr, 1977) 178-181; Ernst Benz, *Swedenborg in Deutschland: F. C. Oetingers und Immanuel Kants Auseinandersetzung mit der Person und Lehre Emanuel Swedenborgs* (Frankfurt/M: Vittorio Klostermann, 1947) 37 ff.

[13] "Da sind die sinnliche Vorstellungen lauter jüdische Wortspiele; und diß ist der Hauptirrthum unserer Zeit. Man muß ganz anderst denken, und den wörtlichen Ausdruck Christi in den Propheten [sic!] nicht von der Sinnlichkeit ausleeren." (*BEW*, Vorrede [6v])

[14] "Herr Ober-Consistorial-Rath Teller nimmt sich viel heraus seinen Haß wider alles Sinnliche zu äussern. Er leert nicht nur die Worte der Schrift aus, sondern er verdreht sie. Das Fundament ist, daß er das Sinnliche vor Einbildung hält." (*BEW* 67)

[15] "Geist ist etwas eingewickeltes, Sinn ist eine Auswicklung, Auseinanderlegung dessen, was aus dem innersten Punct sich ausbreitet." (*BEW* 28)

This nexus of sensate meaning is precisely what Oetinger misses in Teller's dictionary:

> Teller will eine leichte Gerechtigkeit einführen, er will die Religion von den falschen Vergnügungen der Einbildungs-Kraft an sinnlichen Bildern loß machen, aber er sieht nicht hinaus, daß das Sinnliche der Schrift die Hauptsache ist. (*BEW* 260)

The contrast to Teller is indeed striking. In his foreword to the third edition[16] of the *Wörterbuch* Teller writes that the biblical exegete should extract a general principle from the sensate language or tropes in the Bible:

> Nun die Apostel wechseln so mit den bildlichen Darstellungen Christi ab, als eines Lammes, welches geschlachtet, als Opfers, welches dargebracht wird und des Priesters, der es darbringt; als einer trocknen Gabe; dann als eines Mittlers eines neuen Bundes, eines Haupts des Leibes, eines Hirten, Erzhirten, eines Königs, und vor Juden, die an alle diese sichtbaren Gegenstände nach der Einrichtung ihres Landes, ihrer Regierung und ihrer Gottesdienste gewöhnt waren, daß sie alle eine Einzige Hauptvorstellung von seinem Erlösungsgeschäfte übrig lassen, wenn man sie gehörig entkleidet: soll nun nicht diese die Wahrheit, jenes alles das Unwesentliche seyn? (*WB* 49)

Teller applies here the "accommodation theory" developed by the Halle theologian, Johann Salomo Semler, according to which Christ and the apostles accommodated the coarse, sensual understanding of the Jews by cloaking moral concepts in sensate imagery.[17] The images constitute merely the *Lehrart* of the apostles and therefore are non-essential, while "truth" or *Lehrbegriff* is found by "disrobing" the images, reducing them to a general, moral concept. Interestingly, Teller justifies this abstracting strategy by drawing analogies to two harbingers of the modern world, the scientific method and a money economy:

> Wenn die Apostel mit tropischen Ausdrücken und Vorstellungen so abwechseln, daß die Bedeutung von allen auf einen Einzigen Lehrsatz angewendet werden kann [...] so ist dieser Lehrsatz die allgemeine Wahrheit, und jenes Bildliche gehört zu ihrer besondern Lehrart nach Zeiten und Umständen. So urtheilt man in der Physik: man hält die Hypothese für die wahrscheinlichste, mit welcher die meisten Phänomenen übereinstimmen. (*WB* 48-49)

In the same passage Teller continues with another analogy:

---

[16] This edition appeared in 1780; the forewords to all previous editions are included in the 1792 edition I am using. The foreword of the third edition, from which the quotations in my text below are drawn, is particularly useful here because of its reflections on the hermeneutical principles Teller applied in the *WB*. Although this edition appeared after Oetinger's *BEW*, I have cited from the foreword in outlining Teller's hermeneutical position, since it does not go beyond the hermeneutical practice of the first edition.

[17] In the foreword to the third edition of the *Wörterbuch* Teller acknowledges his debt to Semler (*WB* 42).

Lehrart, das begreife ich sehr wohl, verschiedene Vorstellungsart der Religionsweisheit wird immer bleiben und bleiben müssen. Wer kann das gute edle Metall ohne Zusatz mit geringerm verarbeiten und welcher Geldliebende hält nicht dem ungeachtet sein Gold werth? Aber wenn dieses Zusatzes zu viel wird, wenn dadurch die in einem Lande gangbare Münze über die Helfte des innern Werths verliert, daß wilder Streit darüber in Handel und Wandel entsteht, und Kenner die geringhaltige Münze doch durchaus für vollwichtig annehmen sollen; können und werden diejenigen, die noch ein Wort sprechen dürfen, sich nicht darüber laut beschweren? (*WB* 50-51)

Just as the scientist privileges hypotheses that can be most broadly generalized, and just as a money economy requires a universal monetary standard, so, Teller argues, correct exegesis must subject the plethora of sensate images to a universally valid language — that of moral philosophy. While Teller's employment of analogy to "illustrate" his point suggests to the modern reader that his own thought has remained suspiciously entangled within the nexus of sensate language,[18] the analogies do serve to transfer the validity that science and commerce were acquiring in the 18th century, as privileged sites of truth, value, and power, to Teller's biblical hermeneutics.

While Teller supports his "geometrical" hermeneutics with the tools of modernism, Oetinger anchors the "generative" method in what by this time was a dying tradition of emblematics, and in the archaic hermetic sciences, particularly alchemy. Both emblematics and alchemy are closely linked in Oetinger's mind. He appropriates relatively few conventional emblems in the *BEW*, but rather is interested in the underlying emblematic assumption that correspondences exist between the physical and spiritual world. In the context of Oetinger's theology, biblical emblems serve to demonstrate the principle of *Geistleiblichkeit*: the plethora of emblems generated by biblical concepts is an expression of the drive of the spirit to specify itself in a manifold of physical forms. Biblical emblems need not even be strictly inter-biblical in their reference. At times the exegete must interpret them "aus der ganzen Analogie oder Aussicht in das System" (*BEW* 837), as is the case with Samson's riddle in Judges 14:14. Samson had killed a lion in whose carcass a swarm of bees subsequently nested and produced honey; he invented the following riddle based on this incident: "Out of the eater came what is eaten, and out of the strong came what is sweet." The riddle's meaning must be determined "aus der Analogie der Chemie [i.e. alchemy]" (*BEW* 838), states Oetinger: drawing honey from the lion corresponds to drawing sweetness from salt (an alchemical process), which corresponds to Jesus Christ drawing glory, life, and

---

[18] Teller betrays a vague awareness of this entanglement at the conclusion of his discussion of the analogies: "Ich will mich ohne Bild erklären." (*WB* 51)

immortality from death.[19] Understood from "the whole system" of Oetinger's theosophy, the riddle presents in emblematic or sensate form the most central concern of alchemy: the principle of spiritual regeneration, which Oetinger believes is at work in the progressive corporealization of God throughout history.

Emblems thus have an eschatological perspective in Oetinger's thought. Emblematic correspondences constitute physical connections generated by an eschatologically transmuting physico-spiritual life force within the world. The exegete of emblems recognizes the "form" within the "mass" and can anticipate to some degree how this form will be reembodied in the future world:

> Die sinnbildliche Art zu reden läßt sich nicht allemal aus der vorliegenden Masse, sondern aus der Gestalt, so die Masse hat, denken. Nun ist die Form und die Masse an sich nur ein Ding, aber die Form muß man in Gedanken abziehen und denken, es werde in künftiger Welt die ganze Gestaltung der neu erschaffenen Dingen etwas anderst als jetzt dargelegt werden; alsdenn muß man die ganze Form der zukünftigen Dinge, so viel die Schrift davon zerstreut sagt, vor Augen haben und denken: Es müsse inzwischen sinnbildlich genommen werden, weil wir keine anschauende Erkanntniß von dem System der zukünftigen Welt haben und doch vieles davon im Glauben sehen, weil der Glaube eigentlich eine Darstellung der gehoften Dinge und eine Ueberzeugung von Geschäften, die im Unsichtbaren vorgehen, ist. (*BEW* 842-3)

Oetinger recommends abstracting from the emblem, not following the neologians' assumption that ideas stripped of their sensate "cloaks" are true, but in order to discover the "form," the generative "spiritual" kernel within the "mass," or sensuous embodiment of the emblem. The believer can see these future things in faith, because the language of faith is emblematic; it signifies visible objects which, although as yet untransformed, nevertheless are connected to the future things through the generative kernel of divine life within them.[20] A parallel can be drawn here to discussions concerning natural vs. arbitrary signs in the latter half of the 18th century, and the growing sense that natural signs conveyed intuitive knowledge which was at once archaic and anticipatory[21] — a key

---

[19] "Es ist dieses Rätzel der Grund der ganzen Chemie, da man aus der schärffsten Bitterkeit die höchste Süssigkeit, aus dem Gift Arzney und aus dem Tod Leben zieht, wie JEsus Christus aus dem Tot, Herrlichkeit, Leben und Unsterblichkeit hervorgebracht zur Versönung für unsere Sünden und zur Erhöhung deß Irrdischen ins Himmlische." (*BEW* 840) In the *Lehrtafel* this riddle is combined with the cabalistic sephirot: sweetness and bitterness correspond to Gedulah (or Hesed) and Gebura (Din), respectively (*Lehrtafel* 1: 92).

[20] On the forward perspective of Oetinger's emblems, see Rainer Piepmeier, *Aporien des Lebensbegriffs seit Oetinger*, Symposion 58 (Munich/Freiburg: Karl Alber, 1978) 84.

[21] David Wellbery comments on this process: "In poetry those natural signifying procedures predominate which are at the origin of language and culture [...]. Enlightenment aesthetics — seeking perhaps a substitute for the lost Word of revelation — isolates poetic language as a privileged form of linguistic representation, an ideal transparency. In so doing, it ascribes to poetic

development in the rise of aesthetics and the subsequent valorization of poetic language. Oetinger expanded the notion of biblical emblems to encompass all of reality: the book of nature, too, is an emblem book which must be interpreted according to the same generative method as Scripture, and with the same assumptions concerning its eventual *Geistleiblichkeit*. Oetinger called this all-encompassing science "theologia emblematica." This science, an eclectic combination of alchemy, Böhme, the cabala, and emblematics, is both ancient and eschatological knowledge. Practiced by the ancient philosophers and the Old Testament priests, it was all but forgotten as the geometrical method asserted itself, says Oetinger, but was entrusted to a line of alchemical adepts — "Melchizidechian priests" — and seemed to be reemerging in Oetinger's own day. Oetinger reports enthusiastically about the alchemical experiments being performed by a Rosicrucian society in Amsterdam[22] and believes they represent partial disclosures of the coming *theologia emblematica*. In its perfected form in the "golden age," or millennium, Oetinger believed the *theologia emblematica* would bring about the unification of all sciences.[23] At once a science of nature and a universal hermeneutics, the *theologia emblematica* constitutes a polemical response to the specialization and particularization of learning that Oetinger was observing in his own time.[24]

According to the *theologia emblematica* the whole nexus of reality, including all the sciences and theology, is grasped simultaneously and intuitively. Thus the generative structure of Oetinger's hermeneutics requires a corresponding genera-

---

semiosis a double significance, at once archaic and utopian: poetry at once recuperates the immediacy and richness of the origins of culture and anticipates the culture's ultimate goal." (*Lessing's Laocoon: Semiotics and Aesthetics in the Age of Reason* [Cambridge: Cambridge UP, 1984] 83, 84.)

[22] "Sie können regenerationem Plantarum und die 6 Tagwerke im Glas zeigen." Oetinger prays for them: "GOtt gebe ihnen einen Sinn, daß sie die neutestamentliche Grund-Begriffe mit ihrer hohen Wissenschaft verbinden, und zur Theologia emblematica das Ihre beitragen" (*BEW* 837). Reinhard Breymayer has brought this connection to the Amsterdam Rosicrucians, identified in the *BEW* only as "eine Societé in Amsterdamm," to light; see "Fr. Chr. Oetingers Theologia Emblematica," *Lehrtafel* 1: 9 ff.

[23] "Das Jus wird aus der Theologie fliessen, und die Medicin wird nichts seyn, als eine Theologia emblematica, nemlich, man wird an Seelen und Leibern, an Kräutern, Thieren und Steinen die Abbildungen aller Kräften der Wesenheiten in dem einigen Grund, woraus alles gehet, sehen." Fr. Chr. Oetinger, *Die güldene Zeit oder Sammlung wichtiger Betrachtungen von etlichen Gelehrten zur Ermunterung in diesen bedenklichen Zeiten zusammen getragen*, 3 vols. (Frankfurt, Leipzig, 1759-1761) 1: 85.

[24] "Die Priester alten Testaments waren Juristen, Medici und Theologi zugleich, jetziger Zeit aber sind die Wissenschaften zerrissen, so daß kein Priester neuen Testaments an die Wissenschaften der alten hinreicht." (*BEW* 474) "Denn die Zerreissung der Wissenschaften ist eine Folge der verderbten Zeit, die Vereinigung der Wissenschaften gehört zur Vorbereitung auf die güldene Zeit." (*Güldene Zeit* 1: 14)

tive epistemology. Oetinger theorized about a human faculty capable of perceiving according to the generative method; he called it the *sensus communis*.[25] The *sensus communis* knows through the senses — both the five senses and an "inner sense" — rather than through the reason; it knows simultaneously and intuitively rather than analytically and logically. In defining this concept Oetinger was in step with contemporaries who advocated as a corrective to Wolff the faculty of feeling, or *Empfindung*, as an independent faculty of the soul.[26] The privileging of sensate over rational cognition signals the rise of philosophical aesthetics in the latter half of the 18th century; again we can see parallels between Oetinger and anti-Wolffian intellectual currents that flowed into the aesthetic philosophy of the Romantics.

Teller's hermeneutics is based on a polarity light versus dark, of reason versus the senses, where the latter pole must systematically be excluded from proper exegesis. The contrast to Oetinger is striking: applying the model of cabalistic dynamism to his hermeneutics, the forces of darkness and light interact within the word, from which arises its semantic vitality:

> Es werden bei den Sinnbildern viele Contraria, wie Licht und Schatten angebracht [...] da der Schatten das Licht erhöhen muß. Daher muß man die Dissonanz zur Consonanz bringen, wie in der Music oder wie in der Perspectiv-Kunst, da der Schatten die Sache viel natürlicher, als wenn alles einerley wäre, vorbildet. Folglich muß der Bezug der Verschiedenheit oder Diversité in eine Conformité ausgehen, da muß nicht einerlei zu einerlei, sondern vielerlei mit viel Gegensätzen zu einer Einförmigkeit gebracht werden. (*BEW* 843)

Teller's exegesis, on the other hand, strives for this univocal "einerlei zu einerlei" rejected by Oetinger, where ratio meets rational meaning in specular, sexless[27]

---

[25] Oetinger's most thorough treatment of this faculty is in his *Inquisitio in sensum communem et rationem* (1753; Stuttgart-Bad Cannstatt: Friedrich Frommann, 1964); see also Oetinger's *Die Warheit des SENSVS COMMVNIS oder des allgemeinen Sinnes, in dem nach dem Grundtext erklärten Sprüchen und Prediger Salomo* [...] (Tübingen: Fues, 1781). Gadamer takes up Oetinger in his *Wahrheit und Methode* as an advocate of a kind of cognition outside the domain of rational thought, and places him along with other advocates of the *sensus communis* (Vico, Shaftesbury) in a tradition which leads to the understanding of aesthetic experience as a source of truth (*Gesammelte Werke*, 7 vols. [Tübingen J.C.B. Mohr, 1986-1991] 1: 32 ff).

[26] Guntram Spindler has suggested Oetinger was familiar with Johann Georg Sulzer's treatises on the faculties of the soul, and that they might well have influenced him in writing his "Gedanken von den zwo Fähigkeiten zu empfinden und zu erkennen, und dem daraus zu bestimmenden Unterschiede der Genien" (Frankfurt/M, Leipzig, 1775), which Oetinger submitted to the Berlin Academy in answer to the prize question, formulated by Sulzer in 1773, "Examen des deux facultés primitives de l'âme, celle de connoître et celle de sentir." ("Oetinger und die Erkenntnislehre der Schulphilosophie des 18. Jahrhunderts," *Pietismus und Neuzeit* 10 [1984]: 43-46.)

[27] We can sense something of Teller's distaste for sexual imagery. Under the entry "Braut, Bräutigam," Teller writes: "Man sollte also Jesum nicht in das Spiel mengen, welches man zuweilen mit der Kirche, als seiner Braut, treibt. [...] Ich bestimme diese Anmerkung besonders

contemplation. Oetinger's exegesis of the "pregnant" word, by contrast, is predicated on the attraction and repulsion of opposites by which spirit becomes incarnate. The science of the reason, logic, thus is inadequate in interpreting the *geistleiblich* word:

> GOtt will nemlich die syllogistische Ordnung der Gedanken nicht aufheben, sondern beleben. Gal. 3,21. Dazu hat er die Anstalt der Gnade im Evangelio gegeben Röm. 4,21. Die Logic ist nicht die Anstalt dazu, sondern nur ein Gesez, nach welchem Niemand Consequent wandelt. In etlichen Stücken bringt sie eine Maschinen mäsige Form der Gedanken zuwegen. Aber im Evangelio muß jeder reeller Gedank nicht nur geformt, sondern gebohren werden. (*BEW* 282)

The "real thoughts" of the Gospel are *born*, not formed, says Oetinger, suggesting that meaning arises not through deduction or analysis, but through the interaction of divine forces at work in the process of life itself.

In formulating a hermeneutics in opposition to Wolffian rationalism, Oetinger aligned himself with thinkers and traditions outside the mainstream of the Enlightenment. While the mainstream typically discredited Jewish scriptures and practices as being sensual, servile or impure,[28] Oetinger considered the sensate quality of the "Ebräische Sprache" the mark of its divinity, and sought out Jewish scholars to assist him with his biblical exegesis. The same can be said of his interest in alchemy, Jacob Böhme, emblematics, and such unusual figures as Swedenborg: in each case Oetinger was drawn to a system of thought that configured the relationship between spirit and flesh as a dynamic unity, rather than dualistically, as in Leibnizian or Wolffian philosophy.

Oetinger represents a vital undercurrent of thought within the 18th century that responded critically to tendencies within the Enlightenment, and which emerged in a new, but recognizably similar form in the natural philosophy and aesthetics

---

Lehrern der Gemeinen, die solchen Tändeleyen mit gewissenhaften Ernst entgegen arbeiten sollten, und nicht die Einbildungskraft ihrer Zuhörer mit Bildern anfüllen, die von vielen gar zu leicht auf eine anstößige Weise erweitert werden können, und sehr oft, auch von ganzen Gemeinen, sind erweitert worden." (*WB* 118)

[28] Accommodation theory presupposes that the Jewish mind was bound to sensate representations, in contrast to the Enlightened age, where rational truths in "pure" form could be grasped. Teller's diction underscores this point. For example, ascribing affective qualities such as wrath to God, says Teller, occurs as a "Bequemung nach den Begriffen eines zu mehr geistiger Denkungsart noch nicht erhobenen Volks" (*WB* 43). The introduction of Christianity as a religion "des Herzens und des Wandels" served to do away with "solche knechtische Gottesdienste" of the Jews (*WB* 124). Under his entry on "faith" Teller concludes: "die Apostel, indem sie das Christenthum selbst den Glauben nannten, [thaten] es allezeit im Gegensatz gegen die jüdische Religion [...], die es mehr mit sinnlichen Gegenständen zu thun hatte" (*WB* 286). This application of a flesh/spirit dualism to Judaism vs. rational religion is widespread within the mainstream of the Enlightenment; Lessing's diction with respect to the Jewish faith in the "Erziehung des Menschengeschlechts" is a well known example (the Israelites of the Old Testament are "roh": §11, 16, 18, 20, 27; "ungeschliffen": §8; "verwildert": §8).

of Goethe and the early Romantics.[29] A range of fascinating parallels can be drawn to Oetinger's thought. His high estimation of sensate, intuitive cognition has its parallel in the developing science of aesthetics as it arose in the latter half of the eighteenth century. Oetinger's generative method also bears similarities to the organic understanding of the artwork put forward by Herder, Goethe, and the Romantics. Thus we can find suggestive similarities between, for example, the Goethean symbol, Schelling's view of the artwork, Hölderlin's poetic theory, and Oetinger's generative method, their common assumption being that certain linguistic forms manifest the same nexus and semantic plenitude that is found in nature. Goethe, the Romantics and Oetinger also all drew on hermetic traditions in formulating a unified view of the world that stressed the interaction rather than the opposition between spirit and the physical world.

I cannot treat the very complicated question of influence in this limited context. In order to do so one must consider not just intellectual parallels, but the social and political setting of Württemberg pietism, which on closer examination presents a number of significant obstacles that would have hindered the mediation of this thought to, for example, the young seminarians Hegel, Hölderlin and Schelling studying in Tübingen.[30] I believe it is most helpful, however, to place Oetinger within a tradition of hermetic and theosophical thought to which many intellectuals in the second half of the 18th century turned to find a corrective to the rationalistic Wolffian philosophy of the German Enlightenment, a tradition that the Romantic generation would also find useful in "overcoming" Kant. Oetinger is one example of a highly original application of this thought within the intellectual parameters of Württemberg pietism. Others came to similar insights, drawing at least in part on the same intellectual traditions, and sharing Oetinger's concern to rehabilitate sensuality. The relationship between "late pietism," as

---

[29] Rolf Christian Zimmermann (*Das Weltbild des jungen Goethe: Studien zur hermetischen Tradition des deutschen 18. Jahrhunderts*, 2 vols. [Munich: Wilhelm Fink, 1969, 1979]) makes repeated reference to Oetinger as a source of hermetic thought for the young Goethe. A number of studies have argued, I believe too strongly, that Oetinger's speculative theology directly influenced Hegel, Schelling and Hölderlin in the formulation of their philosophies: Robert Schneider, *Schellings und Hegels schwäbische Geistesahnen* (Würzburg-Anmühle: Konrad Triltsch, 1938); Ulrich Gaier, *Der gesetzliche Kalkül: Hölderlins Dichtungslehre*, Hermea, N.S. 14 (Tübingen: Mohr, 1962); Gaier later qualified Oetinger's importance, "Zur Tradition von Hölderlins 'kalkulablem Gesetz'," *Schwäbische Heimat* 4 (1969): 293-301; Meinhard Prill, *Bürgerliche Alltagswelt und pietistisches Denken im Werk Hölderlins: Zur Kritik des Hölderlin-Bildes von Georg Lukacs* (Tübingen: Niemeyer, 1983); Walter Dierauer, *Hölderlin und der spekulative Pietismus Württembergs: Gemeinsame Anschauungshorizonte im Werk Oetingers und Hölderlins* (Zurich: Juris, 1986), see my review, *Suevica* 4 (1987): 123-127.

[30] In my study, "Hölderlin in the Context of Württemberg Pietism" (Diss. Washington U, 1988), I discuss the problems involved in asserting the influence of Württemberg pietism on Hölderlin. See also my article, "New and Old Histories: The Case of Hölderlin and Württemberg Pietism," forthcoming in *CLIO*.

Martin Brecht[31] has termed it, and intellectual currents in late 18th-century Germany, has yet to be fully articulated. That such disparate conclusions as Oetinger's christocentric, alchemical eschatology and the Romantics' view of the autonomy of art could be drawn from common intellectual premises is indicative of the tremendous shifts occurring at this time in the configuration of the spiritual and secular realms.

---

[31] "Der Spätpietismus — ein vergessenes oder vernachlässigtes Kapitel der protestantischen Kirchengeschichte," *Pietismus und Neuzeit* 10 (1984): 124-151.

Charlotte M. Craig

Nicolai and the Occult

CHRISTOPH FRIEDRICH NICOLAI is best known to posterity as one of the leading *Aufklärer* of Berlin, an able, prominent booktrader, a reviewer and publisher of high ethical standards, as well as an industrious, much read author.

On the debit side of the ledger, there is hardly another man in German letters who provoked more polemic outbursts than Nicolai. Scorned by numerous prominent contemporaries — Herder, Schiller, Kant — , stigmatized by Fichte in particular among other Romantics, for his "absolute Oberflächlichkeit und totale[n] Seichtigkeit,"[1] he was reviled by Goethe in the *Xenien*, presumably as a revenge for Nicolai's satire against *Die Leiden des jungen Werthers*, and ultimately immortalized as Proktophantasmist in the Walpurgis Night scene of *Faust*. The Schlegels were his sworn enemies, while he served Tieck as a model of a clown in various fairy comedies, particularly in *Prinz Zerbino*.

The neutral position regarding Nicolai's relative merit may be sought in the appraisal of his biographers. Karl Auer credits him with good sense capable of focusing on the reality of the "große Welt," while reasoning strictly empirically.[2] F. C. A. Philips cites Nicolai's *Sebaldus Nothanker* as a not to be underrated mirror of historical circumstances;[3] Göckingk describes him as a socially prominent man of considerable erudition, skepticism, and thoroughness, yet one who remained remarkably unaffected by the German affliction of *Titelsucht*.[4] Gustav

---

[1] Johann Gottlieb Fichte, *Friedrich Nicolai's Leben und sonderbare Meinungen. Ein Beitrag zur LitterarGeschichte des vergangenen und zur Pädagogik des angehenden Jahrhunderts*, ed. A.W. Schlegel (Tübingen: Cotta, 1801) p. 68. Fichte's caustic reference to "Unser Held, [der] ...dicke Bücher [schrieb], unter eignem Namen, und dadurch verdarb er alles" (p. 53), ultimately culminated in the vitriolic "Berliner Badaut" (p.116), a mere "unstudied" bookdealer who took himself as a genuine scholar (p.53).

[2] Karl Auer, *Der Aufklärer Friedrich Nicolai* (Gießen: Töpelmann, 1912) p. 49.

[3] F. C. A. Philips, *Friedrich Nicolais Literarische Bestrebungen* (Zalt-Bommel: Van de Garde, 1925) p. 5.

[4] Leopold Friedrich Günther von Göckingk, ed., *Friedrich Nicolai's Leben und literarischer Nachlaß* (Berlin: Nicolai, 1820) pp. 84, 93, 100–101. This source is hereafter quoted as Göckingk.

Sichelschmidt points particularly to Nicolai's sustained commitment to the common good, which he considered the noblest of all civil virtues.[5]

Memorable neither by originality nor eccentricity, Nicolai nonetheless earned high respect for his demonstrated professional skill, his sense of perfectionism, critical flair and objectivity as the editor of the *Allgemeine deutsche Bibliothek*, a critical publication of international repute.[6] His astuteness, according to Sichelschmidt, contributed not only to his own reputation as the leading *Aufklärer* after Lessing's death, but also to that of the Prussian capital, likewise maligned as unpoetic and intellectually provincial. Thanks in part to Nicolai's critical merit, strong stimuli began to emanate from Berlin — ruled by its resident presiding spirits — Frederick the Great, and the bookdealer Nicolai.[7]

To a much lesser extent, Nicolai is extolled for his relentless persecution of *Schwärmer*, *Geisterseher*, and *Wundertäter*; in his parlance, these categories include Pietists, bigots, and devotees of superstitious beliefs or fears. These were the object of his scorn in descriptive and creative works alike. His particular ire was directed against the Jesuits whom he perceived as vanguard of a new, militant Catholicism, and the Romantics' newly perceived *Träumereien*, which he felt tended to metamorphose religion into a mystical puppet play.[8] Anti-clerical, anti-military, ultra pragmatic, a veritable *Wirklichkeitsfanatiker*, Friedrich Nicolai indeed projected a stodgy image; as a magister artium, member of the Academies of Berlin, and Munich, corresponding member also of the Academy of St. Petersburg, and self-appointed presider of the *Aufklärung* at that point, he would inevitably have to come to grips with the dark side of the Enlightenment — an aspect of the phenomenon which stubbornly refused to evaporate.[9]

Nicolai seemed to favor membership in associations of restricted patronage, such as the *Gelehrte Kaffeehaus*, the *Montagsklub*, the twelve-member, highly classified *Geheime Mittwochsgesellschaft*[10], and the Freemasons, indicating a leaning toward issues which are reserved about disclosure. His essay treating of the accusations against the Order of the Knight Templars and its secret practices and on the origin of the Freemasons[11] is another case in point. Such pursuits, to

---

[5] Gustav Sichelschmidt, *Friedrich Nicolai. Geschichte seines Lebens* (Berlin: Herford, 1971) p. 75.

[6] Ibidem, p. 13.

[7] Ibidem.

[8] Ibidem, p. 123.

[9] Ibidem, p. 136.

[10] Ibidem, p. 74.

[11] *Versuch über die Beschuldigungen, welche dem Tempelherrenorden gemacht worden, und über dessen Geheimnis, nebst einem Anhange über die Entstehung der Freimaurergesellschaft*, (1782).

be sure, tended to serve the enlightened cause because they are carefully reasoned, meticulously researched, and logically refuting the alleged mysterious, casual relationship between Templars and Freemasons.

Nicolai perceived as painful the antirational trend akin to encroaching romantic and sentimental tendencies. In his zeal to promote tolerance, fight hierarchal terror, bigotry, and superstition,[12] he employed his prose work as a sounding board for articulating his fears and his warnings concerning this outrage which threatened to bring about a decadence of chaotic proportions. He felt called upon to vilify the monstrous *Unfug* of Mesmer's magnetism, Gassner's exorcisms, Cagliostro's miraculous cures, and Lavater's defense of all of the above, in an effort to communicate to his contemporaries a message of reason and to encourage among his compatriots a responsible attitude.

Again and again, the enlightener's voice penetrates the dense fabric of sociological, statistical nonfiction, such as the *Beschreibung einer Reise durch Deutschland und die Schweiz im Jahre 1781. Nebst Bemerkungen über Gelehrsamkeit, Industrie, Religion und Sitten* (Berlin, Stettin, 1783). Particularly with the latter two components of the title Nicolai wrestled ceaselessly. In *Über meine gelehrte Bildung*[13] he condemns the teaching at universities of idealistically colored sophistries of "monastic morality" which favors acceptance of the spiritual, "nonmanifested, otherworldly" orientation — a questionable practice highly detrimental to the intellectual development of the younger generation, and an obvious indictment of Fichte.[14]

In his prominent novel, *Leben und Meinungen des Herrn Magisters Sebaldus Nothanker* (1773), Nicolai's campaign against orthodoxy in religion concentrates on the portrayal of the disastrous lot suffered by the title hero, a man of the cloth with a lifelong *idée fixe* about the Apocalypse. His expressed skepticism concerning eternal hell's torments causes him to become disgraced, defrocked, dismissed, and dislodged. In his prevailing adversity, Nothanker is exposed to every manner of intolerance which he recognizes as an impediment to enlightenment. In spite of his destitution and tribulations, Nothanker remains unwavering in his convictions.

Nicolai's personal preoccupation with death and postmortem perdition is recorded in neutral tones:

"Ich bekenne, daß ich nie habe begreifen können, wie man sich vor dem Tode fürchten kann; vor einer Begebenheit, die nach der Natur des Menschen nothwendig erfolgen muß. Dieß kömmt von den groben Vorurtheilen her, welche die

---

[12] Cf. Sichelschmidt, op. cit., p. 119.

[13] *Über meine gelehrte Bildung, über meine Kenntnis der kritischen Philosophie und meine Schriften dieselbe betreffend, und über die Herren Kant, J. B. Erhard und Fichte* (Berlin, 1799).

[14] Sichelschmidt, op. cit., p. 224.

christliche Dogmatik eingeführt, von ewigen Höllenstrafen, vom Zorn Gottes u.s.w. Ich lebe, weil ich leben muß, und thue das beste, was ich im Leben thun kann; weiß, daß ich einmal sterben muß. Es ist eine natürliche Folge des Alters, daß die Haare grau werden. Soll ich mich fürchten vor grauen Haaren?"[15]

If taking exception to questionable, supernatural manifestations, preaching against superstition, hypochondria and other ill-reputed afflictions, were the self-appointed mission of this inveterate enlightener: understanding, explaining, defending or denying repeated incidents of hauntings and apparitions which he personally experienced seems to be an ironical twist of fate and a major challenge.

Nicolai's altercation with his disbelief in occult phenomena reached a sensitive point when for two months and while in full control of his faculties, he witnessed sighting a large number of human and other shapes, including a repeated apparition of his late son along with other appearances of persons living or dead, of his acquaintance.

This unwarranted supernatural experience by one so rigidly opposed to its kind and rationally discounted when reported by others now had to be dealt with soberly. In "Beyspiel einer Erscheinung mehrerer Phantasmen; nebst einigen erläuternden Anmerkungen,"[16] Nicolai regards the concepts of "spirit" (*Geist*) and "body" (*Körper*) as mere abstractions[17] and declares claims of seeing and hearing ghosts as absurd.[18]

Because of his skeptical attitude on psychological and medical grounds he made a point of engaging his powers of observation during each episode and of keeping detailed records. Suspecting natural causes, he immediately reported sightings to his personal physician who had been treating him for symptoms of hypertension and vertigo. Having been under severe strain between 1783 and 1791, which was due to the loss of his son, the stressful conduct of his profession, his chiefly sedentary lifestyle, among numerous other personal problems, he had also neglected to continue the rigorous treatment — the application of leeches to the anal area — customary to combat his syndrome.

Upon calm reflection, Nicolai cited strictly medical conditions as the causes of the hauntings, while failing altogether to arrive at the logical conclusions as to their arbitrary nature: The inability to summon any of the apparitions of familiar identity, to hear noises of their motion, to understand their speech distinctly. He

---

[15] Göckingk, op. cit., p. 151.

[16] *Philosophische Abhandlungen. Größtenteils vorgelesen in der Königl. Akademie der Wissenschaften zu Berlin* [February 28, 1799], I (Berlin, Stettin, 1808), pp. 53–96. First printed in *Neue Berlinische Monatsschrift*, May 1799. Quotations are to the 1808 edition.

[17] Ibidem, p. 57.

[18] Cf. Charlotte M. Craig, "To Hell and Back: Four Enlighteners and the Devils," *Lessing Yearbook* 20 (1988), p. 54.

describes animals and human beings which appeared as being of normal size, perhaps somewhat paler than their real counterparts, but by no means horrifying or distorted. The sightings suggest a dreamlike semblance of neutral but not at all fiendish character. Unlike a dream, however, he was able to recall in detail the circumstances surrounding the hauntings.

Unable to predict or control the frequency or duration of their occurrence, these apparitions continued to persist, even intensified, without warning, perceptible by Nicolai either when he was alone or in company, indoors, rarely out of doors, at anytime of the day.

Upon resumption of the prescribed treatment, the visions gradually turned pale and fragmented before disappearing entirely.[19] A fleeting sensation suggested a momentary repetition sometime later but remained uneventful.

This personal bout with occult phenomena gave rise to the publication of his detailed account which enabled contemporaries and posterity to assess or reassess not only Nicolai's ultimate position on that score, but also his candid admission: Even under full control, man may at times not be master of his vivid imagination.[20]

The essay is enlightening as it serves as a pseudo-clinical record of Nicolai's firsthand, puzzling episode with the occult, as well as his reaction to these vexing phenomena. He systematically cites insanity, a high fever, or a state of heightened imagination — the later being most difficult to trace[21] — as preconditions for experiencing apparitions. Hyperactivity and over-exertion of inventive powers were believed to be responsible in his instance.[22] To strengthen his case he enlists the testimony of similar experiences by persons of integrity while — true to form — he abominates "Wundermänner," such as Swedenborg, for indulging in a speculative and mystic theology, along with heavy foods, and enhancing a system to foster their own reputation.[23]

Ultimately Nicolai diagnosed his experience as having been the consequence of acute illness — a combined nervous and circulatory condition, vigorously disclaiming hypochondria, superstition, *Schwärmerei*, or sensationalism. Having overcome the threat of potentially unhealthy tendencies and prevailed in his rational convictions, he thanked his powers of calm reflection for having been instrumental in restoring his mental balance. Finally, he credited the pertinent views of Kant expressed in *Träume eines Geistersehers, erläutert durch Träume*

---

[19] *Philosophische Abhandlungen*, op. cit., p. 70.

[20] Ibidem.

[21] Ididem, p. 77.

[22] Ibidem, p. 82.

[23] Ibidem, pp. 78–81; 72–73.

der Metaphysik,[24] which questions the serious involvement with this metaphysical knot on the grounds of its spiritual nature. As an object of conjecture, it defies being reasoned positively for lack of appropriate data. Refusing, however, to leave the issue unexamined, Kant declines to debunk the veracity of ghost reports collectively, but rather urges exercising skeptical scrutiny in each individual account.[25]

Undoubtedly, Nicolai's intimate experience with unexplainable phenomena appears to have solidified his reliance on reason vis-à-vis metaphysical issues and sustained his resolve to equate even physical well-being[26] with a wholesome, positive mental attitude.

Quite likely, his critics did not expect an inspiring testimony resulting from his firsthand experience with the occult world. It is astonishing, however, that Nicolai did choose to file a report — an unsolicited admission of confounding phenomena, which he had harshly castigated in others on previous occasions. Baring his introspective tendencies, documenting his quasi-clinical self-analysis, and objectively coming to terms with this unsound issue demonstrate a remarkable degree of fortitude.

---

[24] Immanuel Kant, *Kants Werke*, Akademie-Textausgabe, II, *Vorkritische Schriften*, II, 1757–1777 (Berlin: de Gruyter, 1968) pp. 315–374, reprinted from *Kants Gesammelte Schriften*, ed. Königlich Preußische Akademie der Wissenschaften, II (Berlin, 1905–1912), pp. 1–452.

[25] Ibidem, p. 351.

[26] Cf. August Moritz von Thümmel's description of a journey to the south of France, *Reise in die mittäglichen Provinzen von Frankreich*, (1791–1805), in which he simulates a Berlin hypochondriac who concentrates chiefly on the beneficial effects of the mere change of scenery and lifestyle while in foreign, i.e., unfamiliar areas — the change-of-air theory, as it were. Not the *Kurort* (Montpellier, in particular) and its environs, but rather the desirable metamorphosis achieved in the *Kurgast* receives his attention. Thümmel insists that a syndrom which he labels as hypochondria, one which bears close resemblance to Nicolai's, has sent the traveller to seek treatment in the first place: a secondary occupation, an inordinately long time spent in libraries or in the company of doctors of any academic faculty. The only cure of this "affliction" acceptable to Thümmel is escape, that is to say, travel. Even the rarified atmosphere of erudition becomes a workaday routine unless it is interrupted by the creative repose which only stimulating travel can provide. See also Hans-Wolf Jäger, "Der reisende Enzyklopäd und seine Kritiker. Friedrich Nicolais 'Beschreibung einer Reise durch Deutschland und die Schweiz im Jahre 1781'," *Jahrbuch der deutschen Schillergesellschaft* 26 (1982), pp. 104–124.

Edward Dixon

Reason in Revolt:
Christian Heinrich Spieß and the *Tales of Insanity*

THE CHANGES IN PHILOSOPHY, literature, and society following the gradual demise of feudalism in Europe has been known as the Enlightenment in England, the *Aufklärung* in Germany, *les lumières* in France and the *illuminismo* in Italy.[1] Despite the images of light and hope evoked by these labels, it is difficult to ignore the undercurrent of irrational tendencies and events that occurred in the Age of Reason. The violence of both the American and French Revolutions that championed an enlightened cause, namely egalitarianism, contrast sharply with the main philosophical tenets of the period that were dominated principally by reason and moral behavior. Although the Enlightenment did not erupt in Germany in the form of political unrest, the German *Sturm and Drang* manifested an ideological revolution that expressed the same social indignation that swept the intellectual and political spirit of Europe. Both the political and literary manifestations of irrationalism raise important questions regarding the dark and hidden consequences of enlightened attitudes. Examples of irrationalism and social protest in German literature arising in the final decades of the Age of Reason are Friedrich Schiller's *Die Räuber* (1781) and the subject of this paper *Die Biographien der Wahnsinnigen* (1795) by the popular writer Christian Heinrich Spieß.[2]

Writing in the mid 1790's, Spieß consistently adheres to the humanitarian goals of the Enlightenment. His work attests to the power of the intellectual forces frequently described by recent critics such as Werner Krauss, Christoph Siegrist and Klaus Träger to supercede the customary time frame of the Enlightenment's rise and fall in Germany for the years 1720-1785.[3] As John McCarthy has emphasized in *Crossing Boundaries* (1989), one must look at the diversified nature

---

[1] Horst Möller, *Vernunft und Kritik*, (Frankfurt: Suhrkamp, 1986), p. 25.

[2] Heinrich Spieß, *Die Biographien der Wahnsinnigen*, ed. Wolfgang Promies, (Berlin: Luchterhand, 1966).

[3] Werner Krauss, "Zur Periodisierung — Auklärung, Sturm und Drang, Weimarer Klassik," in: *Sturm und Drang*, ed. Manfred Wacker, (Darmstadt: Wissenschaftliche Buchgesellschaft, 1985), p. 67–95. Christoph Siegrist, "Auklärung und Sturm und Drang," in: *Sturm und Drang*, ed. Walter Hinck, (Kronsberg: Athenäum, 1978), p. 1–13. Klaus Träger, "Aufklärung, Sturm und Drang, Klassik, Romantik: Epochendialektik oder Geist der 'Goethezeit'," in: *Impulse*, 3 (1989), p. 29.

of the Enlightenment in order to understand the source from whence later movements drew their inspiration.[4] One may refer to the Enlightenment's social consciousness in order to illustrate McCarthy's point. Many eighteenth century writers including Spieß nurtured an awareness of social inequality and injustice that writers in the twentieth century such as Bertolt Brecht also encouraged. Furthermore, the enlightened approach to literature as a pedagogical means to educate society and inspire social change became a practice of many modern social realists.

The Enlightenment, as an interdisciplinary movement that drew upon the natural sciences, religion and economic thought, was represented by an international cross section of political thinkers, poets and philosophers that include Montesquieu, David Hume, Goethe and Kant. These Enlighteners symbolized an age that witnessed the erosion of a privileged and hierarchical world order and the creation of a society based on egalitarian reform and individual merit. In the wake of the Copernican revolution, astronomical observations disspelled the notion of a hierarchical universe that ultimately contributed to the decline of the ideology upon which the authority of princes rested. In the absence of a hierarchical world order, political authority could be viewed as originating not only from above but also from below, whereby the source of political power gradually shifted in the eighteenth century from kings to the "common man." Spieß also describes the same transition of power in his tales of insanity, but as in the case of the French Revolution, this transition is not peaceful. Rather, it contains a propensity for violence and irrational behavior. In *Die Geschichte von Friedrich M.*, the voice of the people cries for the release of an innocent man, who is known among the townspeople as an honest and hard working blacksmith. Although the people's demands are justified and reasonable, the decision of the authorities to free the wrongly accused blacksmith is not hastened by verified evidence, but rather by the quiet mob assembling in front of the city hall.

Spieß's formal link with the Enlightenment is particularly evident in his lack of concern with metaphysical speculation. Instead of metaphyics, Spieß focuses on the practical concerns of the common man in everyday life. Within the parameters of the "common man's" experiences, Spieß records the polarization of eighteenth century society caused by social segregation and religious intolerance. More importantly, he describes the impact of these societal ills on the individual's pursuit of happiness and right to self-determination. Representing the egalitarian views of the Enlightenment, Spieß's protagonists find themselves caught in a bitter struggle with society's conservative impulses to maintain the status quo. Ultimately, their insanity is not the result of misguided passion or excessive emotions,

---

[4] John A. McCarthy, *Crossing Boundaries. A History of Essay Writing in Germany*, (Philadelphia: University of Pennsylvania Press, 1989), p. 70.

but rather is caused by divisive social factors that lead them to loneliness and despair.

Just as the eighteenth century scientist required visible proof for scientific assumptions, many Enlighteners demanded empirical evidence in religious matters. Using experience as the starting point, John Locke denied the entire concept of innate ideas and replaced them with human sense impressions. Likewise, Condillac reputiated the existence of objective truth in *Traité de sensations* (1754) by stating that knowledge is relative to the sense perception of each person. Although the Enlightenment's empirical method liberated philosophy from religious superstitions and ecclesiastical dogma, it also stimulated a negative effect by heightening the individual's anxiety with a vision of a universe in which God has disappeared. Although Spieß does not deny God's existence, one feels the absence of His presence in human affairs. In contrast to trusting in God's mercy and omnipotent love, the characters in Spieß's tales feel abandoned and alone with their suffering. In *Ein Haubenstock namens Karoline*, the insane old woman expresses her feelings of uncertainty and disenchantment caused by the absence of divine intervention in the material world: "Wie oft habe ich Gott gebeten, daß er mir's auch so möchte werden lassen, aber er hört meine Stimme nicht, er ist taub gegen mein Flehen!"[5]

Spieß's representation of love reveals an affinity to the Enlightenment's materialism that is exemplified by the philosophy of Claude Adrien Helvètiusis. Spieß does not present love as a purely platonic and spiritual experience. Instead, he depicts love as a physiological need equal to the individual's requirement for air, nourishment and shelter. Although Spieß alludes to the inherent dangers of excessive passion, the fulfillment of love takes priority over the emotional risks. In *Ein Haubenstock namens Karoline*, love and affection are portrayed as physical necessities that when unfullfilled cause pain and mental discomfort. The relationship between the condition and the activities of the human psyche and sexuality is given much attention by Peter Gay in *The Tender Passion, The Bourgeois Experience* in which Gay quotes Diderot's views on eroticism. "There is a bit of testicle," writes Diderot, "at the bottom of our most sublime sentiments and refined tenderness."[6] The Enlightenment's materialism that expresses itself in the form of sensual love does not by any means discredit reason. To the contrary, it is an integral component in the Enlightenment's basic world view that consists of a harmonious balance between rational thought and feelings. In Spieß's *Tales of insanity*, it is not the distortion of reason that ultimately leads to mental illness but rather the suppression of emotions.

---

[5] Heinrich Spieß, op. cit., p. 90.

[6] Peter Gay, *The Tender Passion. The Bourgeois Experience*, (New York: Oxford University Press, 1968), p. 52.

Inspite of his ideological connections with the Enlightenment, Spieß's world view lacks the early Enlightenment's gospel of optimism and belief in reason's power to conquer and eliminate bigotry and inequality. In contrast to the Enlightenment's recognition of this world which Descartes believed to be the best of all possible worlds Spieß's characters experience life as a "Jammertal" of misery and deception. In *Das Krankenhaus der Wahnsinnigen*, the alternate route to society's moral improvement and the individual's perfectability through reason becomes a journey to the asylum. Here, madness appears as a means of escape from the unbearable social and economic practices that interfere with the individual's material well-being and personal happiness. In their madness, the inmates of the hospital are oblivious and consequently protected from the cruelties of reality; in the asylum they live happily and cheerfully with their visions of being wealthy and influential businessmen.

The dilemma of the marginal character in society was not only a topic of interest for Spieß but also for many writers in the period of late rationalism. Wolfgang Promies in *Der Bürger und der Narr* (1987) has analyzed the portrayal of the outsider in German literature and cites as examples Moritz's *Anton Reiser* and Goethe's *Wilhelm Meisters theatralische Sendungen*, as well as Spieß's *Biographien*.[7] In *Wilhelm Meister's Lehrjahre*, however, Goethe overcomes the problem of alienation by making the protagonist's estrangement from society a question of personal choice: Wilhelm recognizes responsibility for his fate and solves his misfortune by becoming an active member of society. In Spieß's stories, the choice is not that simple. The individual's involvement with society is not a matter of self-determination but rather regulated by birth, class, religion and natural forces. Furthermore, insanity is not the problem of the sensitive individual or artist who is out of sequence with society and unable to conform to the practical demands of everyday life as one finds in Goethe's *Die Leiden des jungen Werther* (1774) or *Torquato Tasso* (1807). It is also not the result of a diabolic imagination associated with Ludwig Achim von Arnim's *Der tolle Invalide auf dem Fort Ratonneau* (1818). Rather than focusing on a dysfunctional disorder caused by internal factors such as sensitivity or fantasy, Spieß describes the external economic conditions that strain the individual's rational endurance to lead a healthy and productive life in society. Unlike Werther or Tasso, who are made accountable for their misfortune, the narrator tells us in *Das Krankenhaus der Wahnsinnigen*, "in diesem Gefängnis [schmachten] schuldlose Menschen."[8] Moreover, the reader is also informed that many inmates of the asylum began as respectable members of burgher society. As former economists, businessmen and tradesmen, the characters continue to profess even in the midst of their madness a belief in hard work as a

---

[7] Wolfgang Promies, *Der Bürger und der Narr*, (Frankfurt: Fischer, 1987), p. 230–273.

[8] Heinrich Spieß, op. cit., p. 274.

means to upward social mobility and financial independence. Their inability, however, to be productive and to fulfill their dreams and aspirations is attributed to unpredictable events in nature and society such as inflation, famine, disease and war.

Rudolf Endres in his study *Das Armenproblem im Zeitalter des Absolutismus* depicts the period from the Thirty Years War (1618) to the French Revolution (1789) as a time in which poverty resulting from inflation, taxation, plagues and unemployment encompassed twenty-five percent of the general population.[9] Spieß substantiates Endres' statistical study by representing a diversified cross section of social types. These tales give a broad sampling of the class structure in the late eighteenth century by not only presenting the aristocracy and the educated burgher but also the unwedded mother, vagabond, impoverished nobility, underprivileged soldier and peasant, who become in the nineteenth century familiar faces in Marx's world view; namely the faces of the proletariat.

The attention that Spieß pays to the lower class reflects the changing literary tastes of the reading audience that occurred through the gradual transformation of society from a feudal economy dominated by lords and nobles to a market society managed by the entrepreneur and merchant. The emergence of the "common man's" economic and political prowess created a literary market for popular literature that developed quickly after 1770. This literature not only satisfied the interests of the aristocracy and wealthy burgher, but also addressed the concerns, situations and lifestyle of the general populace. In addition to Christian Heinrich Spieß (1755-1800), other forerunners and authors of popular literature include Christian Fürchtegott Gellert (1715-1769), Sophie von La Roche (1731-1807), Johann Gottlieb Schummel (1748-1813), Moritz August von Thümmel (1738-1817) and Theodor Gottlieb von Hippel (1741-1796). Spieß's *Tales of Insanity* render testimony to the rapid development of popular literature as a vehicle for enlightened ideas that circulated among the rank and file of society. With the growth of this new genre, the Enlightenment truly evolved from becoming a philosophy for the intelligentsia of society to a popular movement that embraced a broad social spectrum.

The spirit of egalitarian reform that gradually changed literature and philosophy in the eighteenth century was essentially non-violent; however, one cannot ignore the possible influence of enlightened views such as Rousseau's idea of popular sovereignty on Robespierre and the Jacobins.[10] Although the Enlighteners did not lead the French Revolution, their philosophy contained a part of the

---

[9] Rudolf Endres, "Das Armenhaus im Zeitalter des Absolutismus," in: *Aufklärung, Absolutismus und Bürgertum in Deutschland*, ed. Franklin Koptizsch, (München: Nymphenburger Verlagsbuchhandlung, 1976), p. 220–223.

[10] Frederick Copleston, *A History of Philosophy VI: Wolff to Kant*, (New York: Doubleday, 1985), p. 95–96.

ideological nucleus that supported the discontent and social unrest fermenting at the end of the eighteenth century that Spieß also shares with his reader in *Die Geschichte von Friedrich M*. As a movement, the Enlightenment trained not only reason but also cultivated a critical attitude toward social pettiness and injustice that spread beyond the eighteenth century through the revolutionary ideas of Marx as well as through the social cynicism of philosophers such as Nietzsche and Foucault. Although Spieß's judgement on society did not equal the devastating attacks made against it by the heirs and successors of the Enlightenment, Spieß belonged to an established tradition of enlightened social critics that included Christoph Martin Wieland, Jonathan Swift and Jean-Jacques Rousseau.

Spieß portrays a relationship beteween poverty and insanity in the tales that is confirmed by the penal codes and practices of the eighteenth century. In *Madness and Civilization*, Michel Foucault describes the armies of beggars whose presence in society eventually became an affront to the work ethic of the emerging burgher class.[11] Having achieved influence in business and government, the burgher developed a bureaucracy for handling society's poor that, in Foucault's analysis, lead to the birth of the asylum. The inhumane conditions of the penitentiary in which the poor, the criminal and the mad were indiscriminately flung together, chained and isolated is described in *Die Geschichte der Sophie G.*: "Die Arbeit aller Verbrecher im Zuchthause war schwer und anhaltend, aber noch entkräftender und härter war die schmale, äußerst schlechte Kost, welche ihnen gereicht wurde."[12] From the descriptions of the asylum, the reader also learns of the negative effects of isolation and confinement on mental health. Similar depictions appear in *Die Geschichte der Ester L.*, where the protagonist experiences in the isolated and joyless atmosphere of the monastery depression and illness.

The insane person in Spieß's *Biographien* also transcends the farcical antics of the simpleton, or picaro, so vehemently criticized by Gottsched in *Versuch einer Critischen Dichtkunst für die Deutschen* (1730). In contrast to the portrayal of the comical half-witted fool, whose purpose in literature was primarily to entertain, Spieß records the details of his protagonists' mental illness and schizophrenia in the manner of a serious clinical case study. Furthermore, the characters' self-reflections provide a critical assessment of the social causes for their dilemma. Ironically, criticism as a process of rational thinking is uttered in the *Biographien* by the insane. In this respect, reason and insanity are not mutually exclusive but rather share a common denominator through their criticism of class and religious bias.

---

[11] Roy Boyne, *Foucault and Derrida*, (London: Unwin Hyman, 1990), p. 7.

[12] Heinrich Spieß, op. cit., p. 256.

Complying with other enlightened literary views, Spieß also practices the principle of probability governing the limits and usage of imagination in literature that Johann Jakob Bodmer outlined in the *Critische Abhandlung des Wunderbaren* (1740). The narrator of *Ein Haubenstock* names Karoline, who retells the bizarre tale of an old woman's social demise and insanity, does not dismiss her story as the contrivance of an unruly imagination. Rather than ignore her, he is fascinated by the possibility of the story's credibility. Beyond the tale's entertaining value, the woman's story performs a pedagogical purpose. From the perspective of the narrative's insights into the social circumstances surrounding her madness, the imaginative mind of the old woman collaborates with reason to strengthen the practical and moral goals of the Enlightenment to uncover and illuminate social inequity and intolerance.

Despite the tendency of the tales to link rationality and insanity with either an individual's ability or inability to function in society, Spieß beseeches his reader to recognize more than simply the work ethic. He calls for compassion and identification with the character, as does Lessing in the *Hamburgische Dramaturgie* (1767). The emotional process of empathy or *Mitleid* that Spieß directly refers to in the tales fulfills an important moral function. It acts as a catalyst that transforms society's intolerance toward individual differences into a broader understanding of human nature and its diversity. Although the desired result of empathy is often forthcoming or arrives too late to aid the insane, compassion is presented in *Zwischen Wahn und Wilhelm* as a stimulus for changing social attitudes that unjustly exclude the outsider form the community.

The issue regarding the essence of the Enlightenment has concerned philosophers from Immanuel Kant and Moses Mendelssohn in the eighteenth century to Michel Foucault in the twentieth.[13] The resurgence of interest in the Enlightenment in the years subsequent to the second World War attests to the significance of eighteenth century thought for the contemporary philosopher in his or her search for solutions to the problems of ignorance and suffering in society. Werner Schneider in *Die wahre Aufklärung* (1974) presents an analysis of Kant's and Moses Mendelssohn's interpretations that reveals diverging and almost schizophrenic tendencies circulating within the same period.[14] In the opening lines of his essay "Was ist Aufklärung" Kant explicitly encourages freedom from societal and institutional constraints in religious and philosophical matters. His famous opening line "Aufklärung ist der Ausgang des Menschen aus seiner selbstverschuldeten Unmündigkeit" epitomizes the age's emphasis on the individual's right to intellectual freedom. The principle of individual freedom in matters of religion and

---

[13] Michel Foucault, "What is Enlightenment?" in: *The Foucault Reader*, (New York: Pantheon Books, 1984), p. 32–50.

[14] Werner Schneider, *Die wahre Aufklärung*, (Freiburg/München: Alber, 1974), p. 43.

philosophy finds an analogous expression in literature in matters pertaining to love. As in Goethe's *Werther*, love in Spieß's *Biographien* knows no limits. It recognizes neither family or friends, church or society; love is autonomous. Just as Kant sought to liberate reason and philosophy from obedience to absolute rule and church dogma, Spieß endeavored to free love from taboos and prejudices. A poignant example of this is the tale of Ester who enters the convent but is later dramatically reunited with her lover in the sanctuary of the church where she disrobes, casts her habit to the ground and flees with Friedrich into the night. In spite of her apparent arrogance and irreverence, the reader is reminded of the oppressive religious circumstances that ultimately lead to her decision to join the monastery. Adhering to church laws prohibiting marriages between members of opposite faiths, Ester voluntarily submits to vows of poverty, chastity and obedience in order to curb her passion and love for Friedrich. Although her escape from the convent involves a serious offense against the church, her reunion with Friedrich symbolizes a moral victory for love and humanity over intolerance and ecclesiastical conventions. Moreover, Ester's action demonstrates that the realization of enlightened goals are often accompanied by great risks and dangers for the individual who transgresses against established laws and mores.

Paralleling Kants support of individuality is Mendelssohn's emphasis on the common good. In his essay "Über die Frage: was heißt aufklären?", Mendelssohn maintained the conviction that the individual must at times ultimately bend to society even at the cost of tolerating prejudices for the sake of preserving the social order. Although the principle of duty does not take precedence over individuality in the stories, Spieß prefaces the *Biographien* with an introduction that recalls the disclaimer in *Die Leiden des jungen Werthers* where Goethe warns against dangerous liaisons, makes the individual responsible for his or her actions and appeals to common sense. Explanations for the discrepancy between the messages of the preface and stories concern Spieß both as a popular writer and a product of his age.[15] As a financially successful writer who enjoyed much notoriety in the 1790's, Spieß was apparently knowledgeable of the ingredients for writing an interesting story with popular appeal that would also satisfy the demands of the censors. His incorporation of the preface demonstrates the eclectic nature of popular literature as a genre which borrowed heavily from many sources including the accomplishments of classical writers such as Goethe. To help further explain the reasons for the preface to Spieß's tales, I would like to cite Faust's famous statement *"Zwei Seele wohnen, ach, in meiner Brust."* Although Faust's declaration does not directly imply the conflict between duty and individuality, it nevertheless reflects a basic dualistic consciousness with irreconcilable tendencies that manifests itself throughout the period in a variety of literary and philosophical

---

[15] Wolfgang Promies, op. cit., p. 259–260.

contexts as exemplified by Mendelssohn's and Kant's definition of the Enlightenment as well as by Spieß's *Biographien*. The difference between the stories that sympathize with the efforts of the protagonists to assert their individuality and the preface that serves as a classical example of the age's general adherence to the Enlightenment's warning against succumbing to passions that interfere with one's obligations in society symbolize the two basic tendencies of the Enlightenment that on the one hand manifest a dark and dissenting Dionysian undercurrent while on the other display an Apollonian wish for harmony, form and order. These dual tendencies may be considered as the propelling forces for the appearance of such diverging literary movements as the *Sturm und Drang*, Weimar Classicism and German Romanticism.

Critics in the past, such as Marianne Thalmann and August Korff, have viewed irrationalism as a revolt against reason and consequently as a reaction to the Enlightenment. Spieß's stories, however, do not reveal insanity as a revolt against reason, but rather as a tragic consequence of reason's revolt against oppression. The view that revolution and irrational behavior can be the offspring of reason and enlightened thought is supported by Schiller in his personal assessment of *Die Räuber*. Here, as well as in Spieß's *Biographien*, morality and equality are controlled by birth and social status. Cognisant of this injustice, Franz Moor cunningly uses the critical power of reason to scheme against and destroy any obstacle to his personal freedom and happiness. Describing the Enlightenment's influence on the play's development, Schiller wrote that it was "das Resultat eines aufgeklärten Denkens und liberalen Studiums." The destructive spirit of Franz Moor, as well as the occurrence of madness in Spieß's tales, are directly related to a feeling of loss and abandonment. Both Franz and Spieß's characters lose faith in humanity, and from the ashes of their experiences, Franz is driven to destruction and Spieß's characters to madness.

Interpreters of the Enlightenment have frequently indicated a close relationship between the rise of the middle class and the growing influence of eighteenth century philosophy. Although both movements opposed the suppressive restrictions of feudal society and promoted political liberalism, it would be incorrect in my estimation to confuse the two as identical movements. Spieß's *Biographien* not only supports burgher society but also criticize its economic establishment. Although the business of capitalism liberated the burgher from dependency on feudal lords, Spieß draws our attention to the negative side of the burgher's new symbol of financial independence. Money and wealth, like Rousseau's description of land in the *Discourses on the Origin and Foundations of Inequality among Men* (1758), are depicted in the *Biographien* as the artifical boundaries that divide humanity. From the perspective of the social evils associated with the emergence of the new economic order in the eighteenth century, Spieß's tales reflect the undercurrent of social pessimism in the Age of Reason which argued that the growth of modern civilization did not inherently imply the development of an enlightened society.

The practical application of reason does not produce in Spieß's tales the desired goal of the Enlightenment; i.e. moral action does not perpetuate happiness and self-fulfillment. The protagonist of *Der eiserne Ökonom* who embodies both the entrepreneurial spirit of the burgher class and the egalitarian world view of the Enlightenment fears alienation from family and friends when he falls in love with a girl beneath his standing in society. The dialectical view of humankind's progress and perfectability through reason is substituted in Spieß's tales with a broken chain of cataclysmic and unpredictable events that brings havoc and horror to the lives of his characters. Missing in Spieß's tales is the final phase of the dialectical scheme in which humanity is transfigured and enobled as one finds in Schiller's *Ode an die Freude*. In Schiller's utopian vision "alle Menschen werden Brüder", and humankind learns through compassion and benevolence to live in harmony with itself. Although the belief in human perfectibility is contradicted by reality and darkened by madness and despair in the tales, Spieß nevertheless directs the reader's attention to the urgent social concerns of many Enlighteners; he reminds us of the bigotry and intolerance in society that not only challanges reason but also threatens sanity. Despite the protrusion of Enlightenment's darker side in the tales, Spieß remains committed to the moral obligations shared by many Enlighteners to serve all humanity. His message of love is the subliminal message of hope in the tales that transcends social and religious differences and unites both the rich and the poor, the sinner and the redeemed.[16] Regardless of the tragic consequences arising in the *Biographien* from religious and class restrictions, the reader should be reminded that Spieß's tales are also love stories and in that lies their ultimate triumph.

---

[16] Although biographical information does not provide an adequate interpretation of a literary piece, it does give us some understanding of the connection between the author's life and his work. Christian Heinrich Spieß was born in Heibigsdorf near Freiburg on April 4, 1755. He grew up in a religious household headed by a minister father and a mother with strong Protestant convictions. After studying in Freiburg, and before devoting himself to literature, Spieß performed as an actor in theaters in Preußburg, Salzburg, Ofen and Prague. His repertoire consisted of playing shy lovers as well as heroic father figures; among his favorite roles was the older Moor in Schiller's *Die Räuber*. Spieß is also the author of several plays, of which are included the comedy *Die drei Töchter* and the tragedy *Maria Stuart*. His most famous play *Klara von Hoheneichen* was performed ten times after its publication in 1792 by Goethe in Weimar. Performances followed posthumously in Vienna in 1811 and in Hamburg in 1824. Despite his notoriety and financial success, Spieß died both penniless and insane at the age of 45.

Anne Leblans

Kinder- und Hausmärchen:
The Creation of Male Wombs as a Means of Protection against the Fear of Engulfment

THE ENLIGHTENMENT'S EMPHASIS ON AUTONOMY, self-sufficiency and freedom as a release of bondage changed man's relationship to women and to nature. Although the enlightened individual longs for nature, he also fears to be sucked back into an existence of childhood dependency on his mother and on mother/nature, and represses all memories of a past in which he had not yet clearly defined himself. The ambivalence of this attitude is reflected in the ambiguities inherent in the German words *heimlich* and *unheimlich*. According to Freud, *unheimlich* is a subspecies of *heimlich*. It is secretly familiar, but has become alienated from the mind through the process of repression.

Why repression? The word *Heim* has strong gender connotations in German. It is associated with what Freud calls "the place where each one of us lived once upon a time and in the beginning".[1] *Heimweh*, therefore, invokes a longing for a return to the womb and a symbiotic relationship to the mother. But since this longing runs counter to the enlightened individual's desire for autonomy and independence, it needs to be turned into a threat.

The association with the mother's body helps explain why *Heim* is related to *geheim*. It would be hard to find a place more withdrawn from view than the womb. Every attempt to reveal the secret and penetrate the hidden room comes suspiciously close to incest, and is, therefore, always subject to the same kind of punishment. It stimulates the fear "of being robbed of one's eyes,"[2] which is, according to Freud, "a substitute for the dread of being castrated."[3]

Although a certain emphasis on individualism and mastery by subjugation is typical of Western thought in general, it reaches a climax with the split between public and private sphere that characterizes the life of the bourgeoisie. Jacob and Wilhelm Grimm — industrious, methodological and highly disciplined — were typical representatives of the German *Bildungsbürgertum* which took pride in

---

[1] Sigmund Freud, "The 'Uncanny'," *The Complete Psychological Works of Sigmund Freud*, (London: Hogarth) vol XVII, p. 220.

[2] Ibidem, p. 230.

[3] Ibidem, p. 231.

cultivating the values of the Enlightenment. One of the crucial factors in the development of 19th century bourgeois culture was the family, for it was within the family that the socialization process took place and bourgeois culture was developed. By collecting, rewriting and publishing fairy tales, the Grimm brothers contributed to the creation of a culture which consolidated bourgeois principles and presented them to the world. "Why fairy tales?" one wonders. Fairy tales recall a past in which mankind was closer to nature. In most fairy tales, the home turns into a place of terror. The association of the home with the mother is very clear, for it is the mother's transformation into an evil stepmother which turns the home into a place of danger for the child. The stepmother (or later in the woods: the witch) is the uncanny double of the good mother. Whereas the good mother gives birth to the child and nurtures it, the stepmother is after its life (she starves it to death or even threatens to eat it). Insofar as fairy tales reveal the ambiguities inherent in *Heim*, they confront us with the return of the repressed. Why, then, are they appropriated by the bourgeoisie at the very same time that it is trying to present itself to the world by a cultivation and idealization of family life?

In this chapter, I will suggest an answer to this question by arguing that fairy tales reveal secrets in order to disclaim them. They tell us something about the enlightened bourgeoisie's fear of being swallowed, but also show the strategies used by the bourgeoisie to protect itself against engulfment. These strategies are reflected both in the way in which fairy tales are collected and appropriated, and in their content.

The late 18th and early 19th century is the age in which the child is discovered. The enlightened attitude towards children is similar to that towards women and nature; it is characterized by the same typical combination of idealization and denunciation. The child is no longer a miniature adult. But if it is not an adult, it is somehow less than human; it is a little animal, a savage, a monster.... Near the end of the 19th century, Strumpell will describe childhood as a disease with no less than three hundred symptoms.[4]

This view of childhood explains the 19th century ideals of education. Educating a child means curing it from a disease and transforming it into an adult. It is interesting to see which form the cure takes. Ironically, the enlightened individual tries to protect himself against the forces by which he feels threatened — the mother, mother nature and the child insofar as it is allied with these forces — by imitating the mother or, more precisely, her ability to give birth. In 1828, Blasche writes that education procreates *Bildung*, but also provides a kind of uterus in which the child is prepared for a second birth. This second birth is, in

---

[4] L. Strumpell, "Die Kindheit als Krankheit," *Schwarze Pädagogik: Quellen zur Naturgeschichte der bürgerlichen Erziehung*, ed. Katharina Rutschky, (Frankfurt am Main, Berlin: Ullstein, 1977), p. 140.

his eyes, a superior one ("Die Erziehung ist nur Zeugung auf einer höheren Stufe, als die natürliche Zeugung zur Fortpflanzung der organischen Wesen"[5]). It is an alchemic process which turns the organic into gold and spiritualizes nature.

It is clear that the concept of male birth contains an element of hostility towards women. Since the mother gives birth to the raw material (the organic nature of the child), she is too close to nature to educate the child ("Der Mann ist daher vorzugsweise Erzieher, das Weib Ernährerin, Pflegerin; denn der Mann ist Repräsentant des [schaffenden] Geistes, das Weib Repräsentantin der [passiven] Natur"[6]). If the mother were given too much of a say, she would spoil the child. It is, in the eyes of 19th century educators, better for the child to be beaten by the father than to be spoilt by the mother — probably, because the beatings prepare it for the life in exile which awaits the enlightened adult.

Since fairy tales are in the eyes of the Grimm brothers and many of their contemporaries products of the childhood of civilization, it is not surprising that the attitude of the collector towards fairy tales resembles that of the educator towards children. Like children, the *Kinder- und Hausmärchen* have a father and a mother. The mother is the storyteller, the father the collector. This might sound a little exaggerated, for there are men and women among the Grimm brothers' informants. There is Frau Viehmännin, but there is also Johann Friedrich Krause, the old soldier to whom they gave their worn out clothes in return for his stories. It is telling, however, that the Grimm brothers pay homage to Frau Viehmännin rather than to the colorful soldier. Their image of the storyteller is characterized by the same set of stereotypes that is increasingly associated with women in the 19th century. Wilhelm portrays Frau Viehmännin as contemplative, passive and quiet. The storyteller is supposed to be close to nature. In Ludwig Grimm's drawing, Frau Viehmännin's mouth is closed and her hands folded, but her eyes are wide open. It is as if they mirror the stories she receives from nature. The collection is a uterus in which fairy tales are born a second time — this time after the image of what the Grimm brothers consider the prototypical German fairy tale. Collecting and transforming fairy tales is again an alchemic process which is supposed to turn the raw material of folk tales into gold. In the *"Vorrede"* to the second edition, Wilhelm Grimm writes:

> Was wir nun bisher für unsere Sammlung gewonnen hatten, wollten wir bei dieser zweiten Auflage dem Buch einverleiben. Daher ist der erste Band fast ganz umgearbeitet, das Unvollständige ergänzt, manches einfacher und reiner erzählt,

---

[5] B. Blasche, "Warum vorzugsweise der Mann Erzieher ist, nicht das Weib", *Schwarze Pädagogik*, op. cit., p. 81.

[6] Ibidem, p. 82.

und nicht viel Stücke werden sich finden, die nicht in besserer Gestalt erscheinen.[7]

The attitude of the collector towards the "folk" and towards the storyteller shows the same ambivalence as that of the educator towards women.

The Grimm brothers' passion for collecting tells us why the second birth is superior to the first one. Collecting provides protection against transitoriness. The spoken word — the medium in which folk tales are transmitted — consumes itself. The written word survives and exercises a certain authority. Collecting is the opposite of letting go. The collector preserves things that would otherwise be discarded by nature or the historical process.

The concept of male birth might help us answer our initial question: Why are fairy tales appropriated by the bourgeoisie and told in bourgeois homes? I would like to argue that the home, as presented in the *Kinder-und Hausmärchen*, and the bourgeois home carry very different gender connotations. The fairy-tale home is the mother's body — or rather: It is the mother's body as seen from the perspective of the enlightened individual who simultaneously longs for it and fears to be engulfed by it (hence, the transformation from home into hell). The bourgeois home, on the contrary, is another prototypical example of a male womb. It is a shelter built by the enlightened individual to protect himself against the dangers of engulfment without foregoing its pleasures. At home, he can allow himself to be engulfed, because, ultimately, his wife remains engulfed by him. As a male womb, the bourgeois home provides protection against transitoriness; it is a home in which people no longer dy. The difference between fairy-tale home and bourgeois home becomes most obvious when we look at their dialectical opposites. Whereas the opposite of the fairy-tale home is the forest, the opposite of the bourgeois home in many literary works of the 19th and 20th century is the city. The forest's relationship to the home can be described in terms of Freud's notion of *das Unheimliche*. *Wald*, originally, meant *unbebautes Land* in German. As a place relatively untouched by human beings, the forest is a primeval world. In fairy tales, it seems at first the opposite of the good and a replica of the bad home. But as a place withdrawn from view, it is also secretly related to the good home. Insofar as it is a former home, it can be associated with the mother's body which was home to the child before its need for housing arose. In the forest, the fairy-tale hero, invariably, finds shelter and sustenance. Unlike the forest, the city is, definitely, *bebautes Land*. Whereas the forest is a primeval world, the city is the birthplace of modernity. As the site of capitalism and industrialization, it is a place from which nature is either excluded or only allowed to exist within the confines of clearly circumscribed areas such as parks and zoos. In the zoo, for example, the enlightened individual can enjoy the wilderness after it has been tamed and swallowed by the city. Whereas the forest is a maternal realm, the city

---

[7] Wilhelm Grimm, *Kinder- und Hausmärchen*, "Vorrede", (Stuttgart: Reclam, 1984), p. 21.

is a world to which only the father has free access. In the eyes of the bourgeois child, however, forest and city are equally mysterious, because they are both surrounded by taboos.

The enlightened bourgeoisie protects itself against engulfment by swallowing that by which it fears to be swallowed. Appropriating fairy tales means transferring them to the safety of the male womb where the danger, embodied by the devouring mother, can be neutralized. By identifying with the fairy-tale hero, the bourgeois child can venture into the forest without leaving the house of its father. Given all this, it is not surprising that fairy tales reveal secrets in a way which disclaims them. One of the connotations of the German word *Märchen* is lie, nonsense.... The fairy-tale world is a fictitious world, a world set apart by, for example, the formulaic beginning "Es war einmal...". Unlike the realist novel, fairy tales never pretend to be true to reality. Although they reveal the uncanny secret at the heart of the bourgeois home, they do not strike us as uncanny as long as they maintain their absolute autonomy from the real world. In Freud's words: "[...] I cannot think of any genuine fairy story which has anything uncanny about it [...]. [...], that feeling cannot arise unless there is a conflict of judgment as to whether things which have been 'surmounted' and are regarded as incredible, may not, after all be possible; and this problem is eliminated from the outset by the postulates of the world of fairy tales."[8]

I will now illustrate how the bourgeois strategies of dealing with fairy tales are reflected in one particular tale: "Hänsel and Gretel." Why "Hänsel and Gretel"? One could argue that it is one of the *Kinder- und Hausmärchen* which reflect most clearly the socio-historical conditions in a pre-modern society. In a time of limited birth control and equally limited economic growth, parents, occasionally, got rid of children in order to secure either their own survival or that of other children in the family. "Loosing" children in the forest was a silently accepted way of killing them. But although "Hänsel and Gretel" is in many ways all too realistic, it does not reflect the reality of 19th century bourgeois family life, and might not have become one of the Grimm brothers' most popular tales if it were not also a warning against regression and an encouragement of individuation and independence. It is precisely this double content that makes the tale so typical. The initial — archaic — content covers up the new — bourgeois — message, and, thus, enables the tale to simultaneously reveal and disclaim certain taboos. Let us have a look at the second content: "Hänsel and Gretel" is one of the only tales in the Grimm brothers' collection in which the transformation from home into hell, from mother into monster, has already taken place at the outset of the story. This does not mean, however, that the good mother is completely absent. Feminists such as Jessica Benjamin have pointed out that the dependency on the idealized

---

[8] Freund, op. cit., p. 246.

mother as a constant source of goodness stimulates the fear of using her up and, thus, of destroying her. She would say that the beginning of the story expresses the "deep anxiety" of the children "about losing access to home, mother, dependency, and nurturance — about being exposed to the cold ruthless outside."[9] In the woods, the initial situation repeats itself in a way which affirms this interpretation. After three days of starvation, the children arrive at a little house inhabited by an old woman. It is clearly their oral greed which turns the originally perfectly gratifying mother (who feeds them pancakes and milk, and gives them soft, little beds to sleep) into a cannibalistic witch. Starved as they are, they cannot resist the temptation to eat from the gingerbread house — to eat their mother "out of house and home."[10] What would be more natural than that she would do to them what they do to her?

The old woman's real or fancied hostility gives the children the right to kill her. After Gretel pushes her into the stove, they leave the house over the dead body of the witch, but not without her treasures. One could argue that Hansel and Gretel eat the witch twice; first, when they eat from the gingerbread house, and, second, when they steal her jewels. Ironically, the gifts of the dead mother prove to be preferable, because they are less transitory. In this tale, burning the witch in the stove is part of the alchemic process which turns milk and bread into precious stones. Killing the mother — typically, by letting her be swallowed by the flames of her own love/hatred — enables the children to possess her without having to be afraid that they will be possessed by her.

Many critics have discussed the importance of the psychological technique of projection in "Hänsel and Gretel," and the *Kinder-und Hausmärchen* in general. The mother's hostility is projected onto her by the children who are trying to free themselves from dependency. If she is a witch, they can get rid of her without having to feel guilty. What needs to be emphasized, however, is that projection also serves the interests of the bourgeois male — indirectly present as the collector, transformer, buyer, narrator of fairy tales — , who tries to neutralize the dangers of engulfment by creating a male womb in imitation of the female one. The shadow of the father behind the children put their quest for independence in a somewhat different light. Hänsel's and Gretel's rebellion against the mother is part of their socialization process in the spirit of the Enlightenment. The element of secrecy in which the fairy tale communicates its message is also a very important component in the way the children extricate themselves from the mother's clutches. Since she is so much more powerful than they are, they need to be cunning. Cunning, which is ethymologically related to canny and uncanny, seems to be part of the whole network of ambivalences generated by *heimlich* and

---

[9] Jessica Benjamin, *The Bonds of Love*, (New York: Pantheon, 1988), p. 205.

[10] Bruno Bettelheim, *The Uses of Enchantment*, (New York: Vintage, 1977), p. 161.

unheimlich. Both children deceive the witch, Hänsel when he reaches her a little bone rather than his finger, and Gretel when she acts as if she does not know how to check the stove. The cunning hero does not succumb to the fear of being blinded (or castrated), but has the courage to use his eyes. Since he transgresses a taboo by using them, he needs to be skillfully enough to hide himself. Hänsel, especially, takes advantage of the poor eyesight of the witch to save himself. According to Adorno and Horkheimer, cunning leads to self-mastery and mastery over outside forces, two accomplishments on which the well-being and survival of the bourgeois entrepreneur depends more than on any other. "Hänsel and Gretel" describes a rite of passage all bourgeois children have to pass through in order to be recreated after the image of the father. Their ordeal teaches them to be secretive, to simulate and to keep things for themselves by withdrawing them from view. They learn how to reproduce the split between a private sphere — which is concealed from view — and a public one, and, thus, to simultaneously recreate and master the conditions which produce feelings of uncanniness.

The Enlightenment's tendency to undercut itself in a dialectics of reversals forces us to formulate the question, whether the male womb is not more of a threat to the child's independence than the female one. I argued that collecting is one way of creating a male womb, and want to suggest that the difference between storytelling and the collecting of fairy tales by male folklorists is one between the ethics of gift giving and of capitalist accumulation. Female birth, which bears witness to the transitoriness of life, can be explained in terms of gift giving. In the 19th century, it is still quite common for a woman to die while giving birth. Every mother has something in common with the Russian sorceress Baba Yaga who uses her broom to erase the traces of her passage. The initial gifts of a mother to her child — blood and milk — become part of the child's flesh and blood. The gifts of the 19th century father/educator — words and other educational directives — become part of the child's superego, but do not dissolve in the same way. Whereas female birth is an act of opening up and letting new life begin an independent existence, male birth is an act of molding the child in such a way that cultural privileges are accumulated and preserved.[11] The *Kinder- und Hausmärchen* already anticipate early 20th century fairy tales of modern life in which the child remains caught in the paternal womb, and the transition from one generation to the next does not take place.[12]

---

[11] This article is part of the introduction of a larger project in which the emphasis is on early 20th-century fairy tales of modern life; there, nature is replaced by technology and the mother/witch by a father/magician or inventor.

[12] I want to illustrate this point by a short summary of "Der Diener", a fairy tale written by Hermynia zur Mühlen in 1923. An English translation of this tale can be found in Jack Zipes' anthology *Fairy Tales and Fables from Weimar Days*, (Hanover and London: University Press of New England, 1989). It is noteworthy that this tale derives much of its structure from "Hänsel und

Since a discussion of these tales would fall beyond the scope of this article, I want to question the creation of a male womb in a somewhat different way. The very idea that transitoriness is something one needs to protect oneself against is problematic. In the economy of gift giving, death is simultaneously mourned and celebrated as an aspect of life. It is because individuation always implies a certain degree of alienation from the community to which one belongs and a disruption of tradition, that death becomes something one-sidedly negative. To a certain extent, the collector brings about what he tries to circumvent. For he preserves things that are already in the process of being discarded. Although he tries to ban death, he is also somewhat of a gravedigger who tries to collect riches on a cemetery. The pieces in a collection resemble the jewels Hänsel and Gretel take from the witch. They are unperishable. Ironically, however, they escape the transitoriness of nature, precisely because they are dead. It is the closeness of the male womb to a grave which best illustrates the dialectics of Enlightenment. Another reason why the male womb is a grave is that its creation requires human sacrifice. Hänsel and Gretel leave the house of the witch over her dead body. Insofar as the fate of the witch reflects that of the bourgeois mother, there is a body closeted in every bourgeois home. A fairy tale like "Hänsel and Gretel" is an attempt to justify the sacrifice by turning the victim into a scapegoat. There is

Gretel." The collective hero of the story is a group of villagers who lead a life near starvation. They are deserted by mother nature in the same way in which Hänsel and Gretel are deserted by their parents. The little cabin in the middle of the woods is in zur Mühlen's story inhabited by an old magician and his son. An important difference with "Hänsel und Gretel," which shows the villagers' lack of initiative and potential for independence, occurs right at the beginning. In "Hänsel und Gretel," the children find their way to the witch. In zur Mühlen's story, they are summoned to the cabin by the magician. In order to ease their lives, he gives them a machine capable of cutting wood: the srvant. The present comes with a warning, however. The servant will become a "wicked master," "if one day he should belong to one person alone." At that point, the tale takes on all characteristics of a typical warning tale like "Little Red Riding Hood." Not surprisingly, the villagers are tricked into selling their machine to a businessman. They are swallowed by capitalism and terribly exploited. Instead of helping themselves, they return to the cabin in the woods. The magician is dead, but his son reads them sayings out of a work that his father has left behind. The tale ends with the hope that the villagers' children will rectify the situation. They would have believed the words of the magician and shared the use of the machine.

In the course of the tale, the villagers, undoubtedly, learn a lesson. But the lesson they learn is the kind of lesson that a 19th-century educator would communicate to his charges. They are not encouraged to be independent. On the contrary: they are taught that nothing terrible would have happened, if they had trusted the wisdom of the father/magician and behaved like obedient children. The old magician sacrifices himself for the villagers (he dies from old age and exhaustion after fabricating the machine), but he survives in his words which immortalize his authority. Unlike the original gifts of the mother — blood and milk — his words are unperishable. But in the context of the story, this also means that they are not really consumed. They fail to transform the infantile heros (that is what the villagers are) into persons who have their centre of authority within themselves. Since they perpetuate the hierarchy between father and children, the magician's words have to be mediated to the villagers by his son.

no better way to discuss the relationship between male womb and grave than by looking at the way in which one particular womb — the collection — is formed.

Wilhelm Grimm's "Vorrede" to the second edition of the *Kinder- und Hausmärchen* tells us something about the collector. One of the most striking features of this text is that Wilhelm describes fairy tales as if they were plants — in other words: as if they were products of nature's fecundity rather than of human creativity. Nature's role in the "Vorrede" resembles that of the mother in fairy tales. On the one hand, it is a source of plenitude which gives birth to an enormous variety of fairy tales in the same way in which it generates an enormous variety of plants and other forms of natural life. Unfortunately, however, this plenitude is already becoming a thing of the past:

> So ist es uns vorgekommen, wenn wir gesehen haben, wie von so vielem, was in früherer Zeit geblüht hat, nichts mehr übriggeblieben, selbst die Erinnerung daran fast ganz verloren war, als unter dem Volke Lieder, ein Paar Bücher, Sagen und diese unschuldigen Hausmärchen [...]. Was für eine innerlich reichere Sammlung wäre im 15ten Jahrhundert [...] möglich gewesen.[13]

Many of us would ascribe the decline of storytelling and the disruption of the relationship between man and nature to historical factors such as growing urbanization and the triumph of capitalism with its one-sided exploitation of nature. But since Wilhelm Grimm ascribes fairy tales to nature, he is not in a very good position to discuss any historical factors. As a consequence, a reversal takes place which reminds us of the use of projection in fairy tales. Nature needs to be protected against man. But, even more importantly, man needs to be protected against nature which treats him in a stepmotherly fashion. At least to a certain extent, nature is made responsible for what man does to it. With almost baroque sensitivity, Wilhelm Grimm describes the inhospitable world in which the modern individual is condemned to live. In the modern world, the coziness of "alle heimlichen Plätze in Wohnungen und Gärten, die vom Großvater bis zum Enkel fortdauerten" is replaced by "dem stätigen Wechsel einer leeren Prächtigkeit."[14] It is the fundamental homelessness of the enlightened individual which necessitates the activities of the collector.

We argued before that the collector transfers fairy tales to a male womb. What exactly does that mean? One of the first things that strikes us is that the Grimm brothers did most of their fieldwork at home. They would invite their informants to their house, and listen to them while they told their stories aloud. Sometimes, they would write down the tales immediately. On other occasions, however, they would write them down from memory a few days later. Even when they wrote

---

[13] Grimm, op. cit., p. 15.

[14] Ibidem.

them down right away, they would store them in a desk or drawer before publishing them. By withdrawing tales from view and then bringing them to light again, the collector stages a ritual of death and rebirth which creates an illusion of distance. The time that elapses between listening to a tale and publishing a written version of it removes the collector from the storyteller/informant and her tale. From the perspective of the collector, the storyteller becomes "uns etwas bereits Entferntes und weiter sich noch Entfernendes."[15] The resurrected tale seems to come from another world. In the published tale, the familiar appears unfamiliar, the everyday exotic, the present a remnant of a by-gone age. The other world, however, is also intensely familiar, for it is one's *Heimat*, the homeland of one's childhood and of the childhood of civilization. Insofar as collecting creates an illusion of distance, *Heimat* is a substitute past. But although it is a substitute, it has in the eyes of the enlightened individual some advantages over the real past. For he can possess it without being possessed by it.

Like *Heim*, *Heimat* is a word with strong gender connotations. In German literature, it is often embodied by a woman who presents a moment of earthly permanence in a time of historical turmoil. Insofar as it is a land of origin which evokes images of immediacy, authenticity and undisturbed bliss, it is a mother- rather than a fatherland. But it is a male creation; like *Heim*, *Heimat* is the mother's body seen from the perspective of the enlightened individual who is isolated from past and future. *Heimat* is externalized inner reality. It is like a screen on which one projects a mythical space which exists outside of historical time. It is a word full of ambiguities. Since everyone is born from a woman, it is to a certain extent everyone's homeland. But it has been put in the service of regionalism, nationalism, ethnic strife, and other forms of intolerance. The ambivalence at the core of *Heimat* illustrates once more the price paid for the creation of a male womb. All too often, *Heimatliebe* seems to be related to resentment.

Which place does resentment occupy in the network of ambivalences generated by *heimlich* and *unheimlich*? First of all, resentment is a form of projection. Although it is directed against others, it results from a feeling of dissatisfaction with oneself or with the constraints imposed upon oneself by the members of one's own group:

> Allein der Groll gegen die Verbote der *eigenen* Gesellschaft bilden den Anstoss unserer Ressentiments gegen unsere privaten und kollektiven Feinde — und nicht etwa deren lästigen Eigenschaften.[16]

---

[15] Walter Benjamin, "Der Erzähler," *Gesammelte Schriften*, ed. Rolf Tiedemann and Hermann Schweppenhäuser, (Frankfurt am Main: Suhrkamp, 1977), II,2, p. 438.

[16] Alexander und Margarete Mitcherlich, *Die Unfähigkeit zu trauern*, (München, Zürich: Piper, 1988), p. 112.

Alexander and Margarete Mitscherlich write. One projects one's own hostilities and shortcomings onto others, and then "forgets" that one has done so. Since "forgetting" is a form of denial, resentment is a sentiment one does not easily recognize in oneself. One is extremely sensitive, however, to its existence in others. Paradoxically, it strikes us in others as an inability to forget. The resentful other refuses ever "to get over" anything. It is the form which resentment takes in others that reminds us of *das Unheimliche*. *Das Unheimliche* is something that ought to have remained secret and hidden, but has come to light. The resentful other continues to remind us of something that should be either forgotten or relegated to the realm of the personal or historical past, but that he keeps alive.

Love for *Heimat* and resentment are ambivalently related. Both are externalizations of inner reality. The inability "to let go," which is so typical of the resentful other, is also characteristic of the collector who tries to create a *Heimat* out of the discarded fragments of the past. As with the dichotomy *heimlich/unheimlich*, it is hard to identify the positive term of the opposition. *Heimat* is positive, but also reeks of provincialism and intolerance. Resentment is negative, but the insights of the resentful other can be useful correctives to dominant views. For the "things" he refuses to forget are never neutral. Most often, they are slights, injustices and deprivations which he experienced at one point or another in his life. Alexander and Margarete Mitscherlich point out that it is in most cases the (former) oppressor who is ready to let go, and the victim who is unable to forget. Since history is nearly always told from the perspective of the victor, the resentful version of the victim is full of subversive potential.

Nietzsche's *Vom Nutzen und Nachteil der Historie* shows that he was one of the first 19th century thinkers to both understand and criticize the need to create a *Heimat*. His antiquarian historian, who is a brother of the collector, finds shelter in the past, precisely because he manages to appropriate it, and turn it into an extension of his present.

> Das Kleine, das Beschränkte, das Morsche und Veraltete erhält seine eigne Würde und Unantastbarkeit dadurch, daß die bewahrende und verehrende Seele des antiquarischen Menschen *in diese Dinge übersiedelt und darin ein heimisches Nest bereitet. Die Geschichte seiner Stadt wird ihm zur Geschichte seiner selbst; er versteht die Mauer, das getürmte Tor, die Ratsverordnung, das Volksfest wie ein ausgemaltes Tagebuch seiner Jugend und findet sich selbst in diesen allen, seine Kraft, seinen Fleiß, seine Lust, sein Urteil, seine Torheit und Unart wieder.[1]

Like the collection, the antiquarian's image if the past is a womb in which the individual is reborn "aus einer Vergangenheit als Erbe, Blüte und Frucht."[17] But Nietzsche knows very well that this womb is also a grave. The antiquarian historian mummifies the past rather than that he uses it to create new life. Nietzsche

---

[17] Friedrich Nietzsche, "Vom Nutzen und Nachteil der Historie", *Werke in drei Bänden*, ed. Karl Schlechta, (München: Hanser, 1954), vol I, p. 226.

also knows that *Heimatliebe* implies a certain degree of provincialism and intolerance towards what is new, foreign or in the process of becoming. The antiquarian's fear of transitoriness manifests itself as a fear of nomadism ("die furchtbaren Wirkungen abenteuernder Auswanderungslust") and cosmopolitism ("den Zustand eines Volkes [...], das die Treue gegen seine Vorzeit verloren hat und einem rastlosen, kosmopolitischen Wählen und Suchen nach Neuem und immer Neuem preisgegeben ist").[18] Nomads and cosmopolitans (a look at 19th and 20th century history enables us to translate Nietzsche's terms in very specific ways) become the objects of his resentment.

Nietzsche's analysis enables us to summarize once more how resentment works. Resentment, I argued, is often a response to an injury. The enlightened individual is wounded by a loss which he experiences as traumatic. He is an orphan in an inhospitable world, longing for a mother (the mother of his childhood, mother nature) by whom he also fears to be engulfed. Insofar as modern man has mastered nature by distancing himself from it, the injury is self-inflicted. The insight derived from suffering could be a useful corrective to the one-sided ideal of progress and technological development. But the enlightened individual tends to experience the injury as being inflicted upon him by an uncaring mother. Rather than taking responsibility for the changes in his relationship to nature, he projects the responsibility onto nature, and seeks refuge in a substitute womb which he himself creates. In order to feel at home in his substitute homeland, he needs to project his feelings of rootlessness and isolation onto others. These others soon become his enemies, because they keep reminding him of certain things within himself from which he tries to dissociate himself. They need to be sacrificed.

---

[18] Ibidem, p. 227.

Christiane Staninger

E.T.A. Hoffmann's *The Sand Man* and the Night Side of the Enlightenment

E.T.A. HOFFMANN'S NARRATIVE *THE SAND MAN* is to this day omitted from a particular university course in German Romanticism which centres on literature reacting to the Enlightenment. When asked of the reason for this omission, the instructor declared the text a failure. Though other Hoffmann stories earned his praise, *The Sand Man* with its "structural incoherences" and its "logical flaws," was declared a "misfit" and a "mess," too unfocused to lend itself to serious academic perusal. I want to argue in this essay that Hoffmann's text as a critique of Enlightenment thinking succeeded precisely because of these incoherences, these deviations from more familiar story telling. In *The Sand Man* Hoffmann draws a caricature of an Enlightenment's assumption that experience can be systematized. Instead, argues Hoffmann implicitly, the individual perception resists logical dissection. In my analysis of *The Sand Man* I will discuss Hoffmann's narrative skills, his twisting, revolving plot which dodges interpretation based on closure and scientific evidence. This belief in the power of the unexplainable can be traced back to Hoffmann's reading of Gotthilf Heinrich Schubert's *Ansichten von der Nachtseite der Naturwissenschaft* ("Observations on the night side of natural science"). I will show how Hoffmann both appropriated and surpassed this highly popular book of the time.

The text of *The Sand Man* centres on young, romantic Nathanael who distinguishes himself from the cast of characters by his inquisitiveness. In two letters to his friend Lothar, Nathanael narrates the eerie story how evil Coppelius upset his life. As a young boy, as Nathanael tells, he and his siblings are sent of to bed "because the Sand Man is coming," and when Nathanael actually hears a nocturnal visitor entering the house, he desires to know the visitor's true identity. In order to uncover this person's secret, Nathanael hides behind a curtain in his father's room. This desire for knowledge becomes his crime. The act which alters the path of his life is curiosity, "Neugierde,"[1] literally the greed for the new. From behind the curtain, he observes how his father and the visitor, who reveals himself as the

---

[1] E.T.A. Hoffmann. *Der Sandmann* (Stuttgart: Philip Reclam Jun., 1969) 6. [All translations are mine.]

despised Coppelius, a much hated friend of the family, create strange shapes and masses resembling human heads "It seemed to me as if human faces would become visible, human faces without eyes,"[2] narrates Nathanael. The boy, distrusting his own observations, hesitates to speak more forcefully, for his disclaimer "it seemed to me" advances the possibility of an abnormal perception, of a vivid imagination, of a dream-like state. From a narrative standpoint, thought, all these devices still reside comfortably within the range of normal story telling.

As the story continues, though, the reader gains the recurrent suspicion that Nathanael is not normal, maybe not entirely human. After Coppelius discovers the boy behind the curtain, he grabs Nathanael, as Nathanael tells us, unscrews his hand and feet, and attempts to reassemble the boy differently. Hoffmann critics, such as Samuel Weber in "The Sideshow, or: Remarks On A Canny Moment," have argued that Nathanael is only imagining the un-screwing. Weber argues that Nathanael only assumes the detachment of his hands and feet, that this assumption results from hallucinations which supposedly coincided with Nathanael's discovery behind the curtain: "Then Nathanael falls into a semi-trance during which it seems to him as if the Sand Man were to dismantle his body and then reassemble it [...]."[3], states Weber. Not so. The text does not indicate a shift in perception at this point of torture which could validate Weber's reaching interpretation. A careful reading shows no signs of hallucination, no signs of trance. In so far as Nathanael, who had distrusted his perception before, tells us of this episode in meticulous details and precise language, it is safe to assume that an approaching trance would have been indicated in the text. If one wants to argue that Nathanael's imagination has gone hay-wire, one can find support in the text, but much earlier than Weber suggests, precisely at the moment of Nathanael's curtain call "it seems to me [...]." After this initial utterance, the text does not offer another perceptive shift within this paragraph. Nathanael tells us how Coppelius discovers him behind the curtain, how Coppelius wanted to remove his eyes, and how only the father's intervention prevents this deed. Throughout this episode, Nathanael's language stays clear, direct, and definite: "And with that be seized me most violently so that my joints cracked, unscrewed my hands and feet and reattached them first here, then there."[4] No "seems" and "might have been's." When Nathanael subsequently faints and recovers, he remembers nothing of the torture. His body shows no sign of bruises, and he fails to comment on the incident to his mother and his worried family who surround his bed. At this point in the story, we are left with two options: To assume that either he is not human

---

[2] Ibidem, p. 9.

[3] Samuel Weber, "The Sideshow, Or: Remarks On A Canny Moment," *MLA* 6 (1973): p.1116.

[4] Hoffmann, op. cit., p. 10.

and did not retain any wounds because an automaton can easily be dismantled — or — that Nathanael imagined the whole scene in a vivid dream, beginning with "it seemed to me." Since he wakes up in a fever, clearly a human ailment, we settle for the last option — for now. Here Hoffmann's plot comes full circle: He introduces a mysterious element which later can possibly be explained, therefore completing his first revolution of the theme of the mysterious.

The unhappy incident is put aside for many years till one day — Nathanael is in College now — same Coppelius, with a different name (Coppola), a new accent and a new profession shows up at Nathanael's door and brings back terrible childhood memories. At about the same time, Nathanael falls in love with Olimpia, a young woman new in town, but he is put off by her eyes which lack warmth and sparkle. Nathanael is deeply disturbed, for he is engaged to his childhood sweetheart Clara.

And now at this point we meet the narrator of the story, an unidentified somebody who had learned of the story, who had access to the letters, and who so wanted to share them with us readers. We continue to hear of Nathanael's life, but the story becomes stranger and stranger as we go. Hoffmann makes the quest for truth more and more difficult. Nathanael's falling in love with Olimpia exemplifies his other-than-human alterity. Coppola appears one day on Nathanael's doorstep and, with a heavy Italian accent, sells eye glasses. His shrill sales pitch "nice eyes, have also nice eyes" terrifies Nathanael. The mention of eyes (instead of eye-glasses) would not terrify most of us in a similar situation; the mix up of eyes and eye-glasses could be explained with Coppola's accent and grammatical imperfection. But to Nathanael, and to him only, these glasses are literal eyes. Hoffmann employs an almost wicked dual narrational perspective when he shifts from Nathanael's point of view to the narrator's within one sentence.

> [H]e (Coppola) produced more and more glasses, so that the whole table began to glimmer and to glisten. A thousand eyes scrutinized and twitched convulsively and ogled at Nathanael; but he could not avert his eyes from the table, and Coppola produced more and more glasses [...].[5]

Hoffmann presents us with two different realities: Nathanael's and the narrator's. The narrator describes glasses on the table, while Nathanael perceives eyes. Whose eyes are twitching on the table? Where did they come from? The mystery of the eyes' origin and nature remains, unless one can accept Nathanael as a robot who (or which?) has extra-human perception.

If Nathanael is indeed an automaton, then he serves as a perfect guinea pig to help test market Olimpia, who is a robot herself, as we find out, an invention by Coppelius/Coppola and his partner in crime Spalanzini. This creation could bring Coppelius divine status and power, and nobody else could better validate an

---

[5] Ibidem, p. 28.

invention than he who is invention himself and highly impressionable at the same time. While courting Olimpia, Nathanael had noticed that his date's eyes were lacking warmth, life, and emotion. Only the binoculars Nathanael had purchased from Coppola create a transformation and make up for her lack: "But when he peered through the binoculars more clearly, it seemed, as if moist moon beams rose in Olimpia's eyes."[6] This phenomenon repeats itself the next night at a ball: While Nathanael had detected a stiffness in Olimpia's movement and a blankness in her glance, the glasses animate her. "Oh! — he became aware how she glanced his way most lovingly, how each sound clearly blossomed in each loving glance [...]."[7] The [Enlightened] critic might want to argue that the binoculars are the force which transform Olimpia for those who look through them. Not so. Nathanael's vision is permanently altered after these incidents. From now on Nathanael needs no binoculars to see life in and into Olimpia. How this new, permanently altered perception came about is not explained. We simply have to accept that it does.

Hoffmann continues to inject elements into the story which cannot be resolved with a rational and scientific system of explanation. When Nathanael one day finds the dismantled Olimpia's hardware spread on the floor, he not only learns that his date was a fake, but that her eyes were his: "The eyes — they eyes stolen from you" screams Spalazini. If so, if Nathanael's eyes were stolen to lend authenticity to Olimpia — the robot —, then when did that theft take place? If we remember, when Coppelius drug Nathanael out from behind the curtain and threatened to take his eyes, Coppelius never followed through, we were told. Could the mechanic have stolen and replaced the boys' eyes after he fainted? Then how did Nathanael recognize his mother standing by his bed when he recovered? And, if these eyes on the floor are Nathanael's indeed, whose eyes has he been using in the meantime? In good Hoffmannian fashion the mystery is not resolved. No explanation, and no hint of hallucination. "Only too clearly saw Nathanael what had happened," the narrator tells us. Nathanael hadn't seemed to see; he saw. The whereabouts of his eyes cannot be reduced to an explanation.

Hoffmann continues to disappoint the reasonable critic in her search for a coherent narrative: Had the binoculars animated the lifeless, they now petrify the living. When Nathanael reunites with fiance Clara, the patient and reasonable endurer of Nathanael's "moods" and "obsessions," they climb a tower to view the countryside. When Nathanael reaches for his binoculars to investigate some distant mountains — why was he carrying these lenses still with him? — he unfortunately aims at Clara. While these binoculars had helped Olimpia to live in his eyes, they transform Clara into a doll and Nathanael into a madman. "Wooden doll, spin,

---

[6] Ibidem, p. 29.

[7] Ibidem, p. 31.

wooden doll, spin — " screams Nathanael, who then tries to throw Clara over the bannister, but finally jumps himself instead. When his head hits the sidewalk, it shatters, we are told. His head could therefore be skull, glass, or wood.

Hoffmann created a text that makes impossible a methodical deciphering. But he upset the rules of how to create a narrative in more than one way. Hoffmann, the Romantic, appears to shoot himself in the foot when he kills off his central figure Nathanael, the Romantic, and rewards the representatives of the Enlightenment, Coppelius and Clara. Coppelius neither is held responsible for Nathanael's death, nor for his father's who had died during the childhood curtain scene, and Clara lives happily ever after. But even though Hoffmann doesn't punish the Enlightened with prison or misery, he sentences them to creative failure and boredom respectively.

Coppelius, we must remember, though off the hook legally, does not accomplish his goal of recreating life scientifically and artificially. His creation Olimpia does not convince the people of the town. The unaffected world — everybody but Nathanael, that is — notes Olimpia's artificial performance. Comically enough, Nathanael' friend Siegmund, while describing whom he believes to be a rather cool, unemotional woman, employs the language of robotics: "Her walk is strangely timed, every movement seems provoked by the pace of a wound up clock work. Her performance, her singing has the irritating, perfect, soulless rhythm of a droning machine [...]."[8] When Siegmund criticizes her perfection, he implicitly argues that the imperfect, not the perfect, is beautiful, and to be able to perfect the imperfect, as strange as it may sound, is the true sign of power. This power still lies in the hand of the divine, signals Hoffmann through Coppelius who realizes same when he attempts to reassemble Nathanael's feet, but forsakes the project which can be only altered but not improved: "It's not right. Was good the way it was. The Old Man understood it."[9] Science and technology, implies Hoffmann, do not improve divine quality work.

While Hoffmann criticizes cliched simple Enlightenment standards, he does not present the Enlightenment as a simplistic set of characteristics. For Hoffmann, the Enlightenment does not stand in a simple binary opposition to Romanticism. Does not Nathanael the romantic fall in love with reasonable Clara? Enlightenment is not merely evil Coppelius imitating God. Through Clara, Hoffmann presents the sunny side of the Enlightenment. Her practical approach to life solves problems, but doesn't dwell on them. "Clärchen," ("little Clara") so her nickname, is a personification of the "Aufklärchen" ("little Enlightenment") when she suggests to remove those thoughts which trouble you. "I ask you, please put the ugly

---

[8] Ibidem, p. 34.
[9] Ibidem, p. 10.

Coppelius and the weather glass man Guiseppe Coppola out of your mind"[10] ("aus dem Kopf schlagen") she begs, a request he takes literally when he hurls himself from the tower. And one could assume she is attempting to trivialize Nathanael's experience when she explains away Nathanael's story: "I think that everything terrible and horrible you speak of is only in your head."[11]

Hoffmann's theme of the inner turmoil as possible illusion can be traced back to a collection of essays which Hoffmann admired and which fundamentally influenced his subsequent writing. Gotthilf Heinrich Schubert's *Observations on the Night Side of the Natural Sciences* informs the plot of *The Sand Man* by outlining the psychology of Nathanael's "illusions." Schubert argues that one, while investigating the human soul ("Gemüth"), might come across another, a higher strain of same soul. "And not too rarely do we see single moments, often brought about by violence, which surpass our known capabilities immensely in spiritual capacity."[12] Although we might see these moments of higher and darker force, we fail when trying to incorporate these moments into our mainstream life. Schubert believes that within each organism, two separate and often opposing natures ("Naturen") come in contact. While one of these natures governs daily living, the other might breaks through at the "highest moment of the earthly existence."[13] Schubert compares this moment with the blossoming of a flower. At this moment, one soul can unite with the other. The flower is metaphorically linked to human experience. Schubert argues that the dark and violent features of a retard ("Blödsinnigen") become smooth and noble in death once the upper half of the skull is removed. This "wonderful, barely fancied depth of our nature,"[14] the "wunderbare kaum geahndete Tiefe unserer Natur," is a mostly positive experience. Schubert's prognosis for the future is optimistic. While the merging of two natures is impossible now, there will be a time when that "which now seems the property of another world, will cross the river and enter the present state of living."[15]

While *The Sand Man* is strongly influenced by Schubert, Hoffmann, as I have shown, doesn't finish along the lines of optimism and Schubert's sense of closure. We can trace Schubert's influence in *The Sand Man*. The narrator shares with Nathanael and Schubert these sensations and forces intruding the body. Nathanael finds peace in death when the skull is crushed. But Hoffmann does not share Schubert's optimism, Schubert's sense of progression. Schubert's hope lies in the

---

[10] Ibidem, p. 15.

[11] Ibidem, p. 13.

[12] Gofthilf Heinrich Schubert, *Von der Nachtseite der Naturwissenschaft* (Dresden: Arnold, 1908 [rpt.Darmstadt: Wissenschaftliche Buchgesellschaft, 1967]), p. 308.

[13] Ibidem, p. 318.

[14] Ibidem, p. 322.

[15] Ibidem, p. 325.

evolution of the human race, while Hoffmann concerns himself with the individual. Schubert trivializes the danger for the individual in his essays. Though aware of it, "the most prominent emergence of this higher urge is only possible in illness, and sometimes results in destruction,"[16] Schubert couches his argument within the rhetoric of an organic whole. And while he illuminates the night side of the natural sciences, his chiaroscuro never questions the premise of the harmony of the whole. Schubert, while describing the undescribable, finds reasons for these depths of nature, while Hoffmann is much more random. Ultimately, Schubert pushes for a harmonic whole in which the individual is merely a part. Schubert's idealism has no room for Nathanael. And his "Night Side" wasn't too dark after all.

When the story ends, Nathanael is dead — presumedly united in soul with his darker, higher side — and Clara moves on with her life. Ironically, the text ends on a harmonious note, though quite different from the harmony Schubert had in mind. Clara's positivistic thinking is ambiguously rewarded when Hoffmann marries her off to a nondescript friendly man — possibly the narrator himself — who provides her with two friendly boys in a friendly country home. The idyllic description of this "quiet homely happiness"[17] reeks strongly of petty bourgeois oak wall units, needle point, and boredom. This is not the harmony Schubert spoke of. This is the life of someone who cannot tolerate stress.

The circle of Hoffmann critics has mostly avoided a discussion of *The Sand Man's* narratology. How much more rewarding is the analysis of madness; how much more reasonable is it to find in Nathanael a scientifically correct description of schizophrenia. Weber's approach, f.i., is typical for this desire to "make sense" of Hoffmann's tale. One misses the point when one approaches a almost modern text with the tools of a rigid "Literaturwissenschaft," which doesn't allow for the conflict of Romanticism and Enlightenment. Everything, they seem to argue, can be explained, must be deciphered. Just this very twist may have been Hoffmann's sneakiest critique of the Enlightenment: Present the Disciples of Reason with a text too hard of a nut to be cracked.

In many ways, *The Sand Man* is a very modern text. It mixes genres, it breaks the rule of traditional narrative, it forces and allows the reader to enter a literary twilight zone, which leaves open the important question: Who is this narrator and why does he know what he knows? The instructor who banned *The Sand Man* from his syllabus must have been looking for fairy tales in which the good man marries the princess. He implied by his choice that literature should not disturb, but reassure.

---

[16] Ibidem, p. 313.

[17] Hoffmann, op. cit., p. 42.

William Crisman

"Ohne alle Überzeugung überzeugt zu tun": Masonic Voodoo in Young Tieck's Enlightenment Novels

TIECK'S LONG NOVELS before *Sternbald* — *Abdallah* and *William Lovell* — have been easy to hate but hard to place. They are easily taken as exponents of the "moral Gothic;"[1] in their sordid schemes to use sons to kill fathers, with sex and loose living as bait, they are usually taken as vaguely admonitory tales of a washed up and derivative Enlightenment conservativism, "the age old lesson of the golden mean" with the eighteenth-century patriarchal gentry as its representative.[2] While it would be incorrect to say the novels have received uncritical attention — three books have been devoted to *Lovell* alone — it is correct to say that this assumption of the novels as Enlightenment works has been little explored.[3]

---

[1] This terminology is drawn from Paul Lewis, "The Intellectual Functions of Gothic Fiction: Poe's 'Ligeia' and Tieck's 'Wake Not the Dead,'" *Comparative Literature Studies* 16 (1979), 209.

[2] Hans Eichner's verdict in his entry for "The Novel" in *The Romantic Period in Germany*, ed. Siegbert Prawer (New York: Schocken, 1970), pp. 66f. Eichner sees the supposed plea for the golden mean as so tired that "most people will be bored by it." This reading of the novel as dull because of its clear "Verteidigung der aurea mediocritas" has a long pedigree in the twentieth century; see Rudolf Lieske, *Tiecks Abwendung von der Romantik* (Berlin, 1933; rpt. Nendeln: Kraus, 1967), p. 24. In the light of such readings, it is always startling to remember that the novel's first readers saw it quite differently, as an unsavory defense of behavior that is "verächtlich" and "ekelhaft." *Allgemeine Literaturzeitung* 4 (1797), 196 f. As might be expected, one strain of twentieth-century *Lovell* reception has been to attempt value neutrality, perhaps most strikingly in Marianne Thalmann's 1970 *Die Romantik des Trivialen* (Munich: List), which sees in the work "keine Bösewichte" and simply "neue Wertansprüche" (pp. 62f. and 106). Such a reading, however, does not abide; while doubting whether Tieck fully endorses a "bürgerliche Lösung" to social problems, Lothar Pikulik in 1983 nonetheless has to admit that the "Glück und Zufriedenheit" of the gentry represents at least a preference in the work. "Die Frühromantik in Deutschland als Ende und Anfang: Über Tiecks *Lovell* and Friedrich Schlegels Fragmente," in *Die literarische Frühromantik*, ed. Silvio Vietta (Göttingen: Vandenhoeck und Ruprecht), p. 123.

[3] The number "three" here is somewhat arbitrary, since it excludes works that are *mostly*, if not wholly, on *Lovell*. The works I have in mind are, chronologically: Fritz Wüstling, *Tiecks William Lovell: Ein Beitrag zur Geistesgeschichte des 18. Jahrhunderts* (Halle: Niemeyer, 1912), to which one should add Fritz Brüggemann's long review article (*Euphorion* 21 [1914], 363-88); Walter Münz, *Individuum und Symbol in Tiecks William Lovell: Materialien zum frühromantischen*

How are they Enlightenment novels, beyond finding happy marriage in a world of living fathers and landed squires better than chasing syphilitic floozies under the spooky lure of demonists?

That these are novels of lure and persuasion is of course common knowledge. What this persuasion is like, however, has been little explored, perhaps because of the novels' supernatural apparatus. In one reader's eyes, the main persuader of *Lovell* — Andrea Cosimo — convinces through "schicksalspielende Mächte" that to another reader appear as an unbelievable somnambulism.[4] Bringing such readings into historical perspective through the novels' French Revolution provenance, a third reader considers both Abdallah and Lovell under the charismatic patricidal sway of Robespierres.[5] Persuading becomes to these readers a matter of spiritualistic mass suggestion.

That persuasion is more involved than this, however, emerges from the complexity of the persuasion alone. In *Abdallah*, Omar initiates Abdallah's betrayal of his father because Omar has been persuaded by Achmed to seek out Mondal, who persuades Omar to persuade Abdallah to surrender his father to execution. In *Lovell*, Rosa initiates William's betrayal of his father because Rosa has fallen under the sway of Andrea Cosimo, who, under his earlier identity as Waterloo had been impoverished by the notorious persuader Oliver Cromwell. The chains of persuasion grow even more involved. Omar's persuading Abdallah is not solely a persuasion of Abdallah but also a persuasion of Abdallah's father away from his belief in humanity, which persuasion is itself an attempt to convince the original corrupter to reaccept Omar back into the original persuader's original persuasion. In persuading William Lovell to betray his father, Andrea is actually trying to compensate for a failed attempt to persuade a woman to marry him years ago.

The vaudevillian complexity of this sketch does not do justice to the sub-persuasions involved in these novels' general persuasions to begin with. For instance, Omar's final object in persuading Abdallah to persuade his father to give up belief in humanity is to destroy Abdallah himself, since the father Abdallah thinks he is turning in to execution has in fact already been turned in — by Omar himself.

Moreover, the novels portray people in a state of positively thirsting for persuasion, as the prevalence of the words "persuade" ("überzeugen") and "per-

---

Subjektivismus (Bern: Herbert Lang, Frankfurt a.M.: Peter Lang, 1975); and Karlheinz Weigand, *Tiecks William Lovell: Studie zur frühromantischen Antithese* (Heidelberg: Winter, 1975).

[4] These opinions are, respectively, from Ferdinand Joseph Schneider, "Tiecks *William Lovell* and Jean Pauls *Titan*," *Zeitschrift für deutsche Philologie* 61 (1936), 65, and Ralph Tymms, *German Romantic Literature* (London: Methuen, 1955), p. 60.

[5] See Gonthier-Louis Fink, "'Was ist ein Leben ohne Freiheit': Ludwig Tieck und die französische Revolution," in *Die deutsche Romantik und die Französische Revolution*, ed. Gonthier-Louis Fink (Strasbourg: Actes du Colloque International, 2-5 November, 1989), pp. 85-87 and 90 f.

suasion" ("Überzeugung") suggests. *Lovell*'s Andrea feels "daß der Geist endlich nach einer trocknen Überzeugung schmachtet," a feeling that echoes across the novel's various classes and situations.[6] Even in escaping his influence, two of Andreas's lieutenants feel "glücklich [...] das [s]ie überzeugt zu sein glauben" (597). The representatives of the morally upright gentry world pronounce as values that "jeder muß nach seiner Überzeugung leben" (560) in a condition of "innere [...] gereifte Überzeugung" (407).

Such a persuasion and conviction remain, however, unstable. Andrea's metaphor of conviction is that of gamblers who bet "so [...] daß sie oft ohne alle Überzeugung überzeugt tun" (683). Indeed, the novel dramatizes such hollow "persuasions," as when Karl Wilmont quite mistakenly says "ich bin überzeugt" about facts of William's upbringing (662), or when Andrea is falsely "overcome" by the "Überzeugung" that he will seduce William's eventual mother (678). In their alternating lust for and dread of persuasion, the novels clearly tie in to a documented, "dominant — and venomous — " sense in the 1790's that the world works according to the rules of involved secret societies like the Freemasons, and specifically a Freemasonry exported from Germany;[7] no coincidence exists in Omar's reaching the ultimate Freemason Mondal through "Steinmauern" (101). Any one point in these interlocking persuasions may be magic or hypnotic, like William Lovell's confrontation with Rosaline's holographic projection, or Omar's sense that Mondal instantaneously opens his eyes: "Wie ein Vorhang fiel es von meiner Seele hinweg [...]. Ich war in seine fürchterlichen Geheimnisse eingeweiht" (*Abdallah*, 108). These instant illuminations, however, have psychological and philosophical preparations that cut into and ultimately critique an Enlightenment world view, and that can be approached only through the novels' more extensively dramatized persuasions.

---

[6] The edition of *Abdallah* cited is from volume 8 of *Ludwig Tieck's Schriften* (Berlin: Reimer, 1828). *William Lovell* is cited from volume 1, *Frühe Erzählungen und Romane*, from *Ludwig Tieck: Werke in vier Bänden*, ed. Marianne Thalmann (Munich: Winkler, 1963). Page numbers appear parenthetically in the text. The choice of this, third, edition of *Lovell* (also reworked for the *Schriften* of 1828) in preference to Walter Münz's great reprinting of the first edition (Stuttgart: Reclam, 1986), might raise some eyebrows; see especially John Lillyman's review of Münz's edition in *German Quarterly* 60 (1987), 672-75, or his *Reality's Dark Dream: The Narrative Fiction of Ludwig Tieck* (Berlin: de Gruyter, 1979), pp. 23 f. Without entering into a lengthy debate about editions, suffice it to say that detractors of the third edition are generally upset about omissions, not additions (cf. James Trainer, "*William Lovell*: Tieck's World of Chaos," *Études germaniques* 23 [1968], 196) and that the question is far from settled about whether Tieck falsified or highlighted his initial intentions of 1795/96. On the side that the 1828 reissue allows "daß der Kern des Romans deutlicher hervortrat," see Karlheinz Weigand (supra note 3), p. 24.

[7] W. Daniel Wilson, "Philosophen- und Schriftstellerkabale: The Conspiracy Theory of the French Revolution and the Origins of German Romanticism (Fichte, F. Schlegel, Novalis)," *Euphorion* 83 (1989), 131.

Both the importance and the instability of persuasion derive from an oddly little noticed Idealist empiricism in the novels. Some link is apparent between sensualist depravity and a radically empirical doctrine of consciousness. Under Omar's coaching, Abdallah intones "daß wir da sind, um zu genießen, das ist die Weisheit, die unser Verstand begreift" (183); yet with its emphasis on what "understanding can comprehend," this is clearly not the naively hedonist misunderstanding of Kant that some readers have seen but a statement about the possible basis of thought to begin with.[8] The "Verstand" terminology, of course, has to awaken thoughts of Kant's "Verstand/Vernunft" distinction, and indeed Omar's abrupt first argument locates Abdallah immediately in the world of Kantian assumptions. The youth wants to understand the limits of consciousness ("was der Mensch fassen kann, will auch ich begreifen"), to which Omar responds with words almost copied from the introduction to the "Transzendentale Analytik": "du vertraust dich einem Meere, das dich nie an's Land zurückträgt."[9] The Idealist conclusion to the desire to know becomes that of self-mirroring: "wir sind in einem ehernen Gewölbe eingeschlossen, wir sehen nichts, was wirklich ist, die schimmernden Gestalten, die wir wahrzunehmen glauben, sind nichts, als der Widerschein von uns selbst im glatten Erze" (6).

The same emphasis on self-reflection as the outcome of attempted knowledge recurs in *Lovell*. Like his counterpart Omar, Rosa claims "man sollte sich [...] daran gewöhnen, die äußern Gegenstände um sich nur als Spiegel zu betrachten" (425 f.). "Alles, was mir entgegenkommt, ist nur ein Phantom [...] meines innersten Geistes," William says. The consequence is one that suggests even more attention to Kant's unity of apperception: "[der] innere Sinn gleicht einem künstlich geschliffenen Spiegel, der zerstreute und unkenntliche Formen in ein geordnetes Gemälde zusammenzieht" (354). Unity exists, but it is an insular unity preserving inner coherence at the price of exclusion from other minds. Here the first impulse to persuasion of the obsessive, Masonic sort becomes understandable. Persuasion connects minds with other minds, and the compulsion to persuading reflects the morbid sense that this connection is in fact gone.

---

[8] A representative statement about misunderstood Kantianism appears in Alan Corkhill's "Perspectives on Language in Ludwig Tieck's Epistolary Novel *William Lovell*," *German Quarterly* 58 (1985), 176. In keeping with the long-standing prejudice that Tieck himself was incapable of philosophic thought, it is hard to say whether the misunderstanding of Kant is supposed to be William's or Tieck's own. (Interestingly, among Tieck's contemporaries Solger — with Hegel's agreement — says that Tieck in fact "live[s] ... in the subject of philosophy." From Hegel's little-read review article on Tieck's and Raumer's edition of Solger's posthumous writings, quoted here from *G.W.F. Hegel: Encyclopedia of the Philosophical Sciences in Outline and Critical Writings*, ed. Ernst Behler [New York: Continuum, 1990], p. 281.)

[9] The celebrated passage is to be found in Kant's *Kritik der reinen Vernunft*, sections A 235 f./B 294 f.

The especially interesting feature of this self-reflexive Idealism is that it does not usually convert to a simple, corrupt pleasure seeking and a stupidly mercenary misappropriation of Kantian ideas. In *Abdallah*, the sensual object, Abdallah's beloved Zulma, remains intrinsically a pure goal, even if she figures unwittingly in Abdallah's virtual patricide. In *Lovell*'s much more blatantly sordid world, characters only rarely claim a debased Idealist empiricism as justification for immoral action, as William does when he say "ich begnüge mich mit der Empfindung" (344), or as the Comtesse Blainville does in her remarks when she praises "die hochgespante Empfindung [...] vor dem Altare der irdischen Venus" (298). Indeed, as the degree of sensualist, immoral corruption increases from *Abdallah*'s to *Lovell*'s worlds, sophistical mention of "experience" becomes much less prevalent. Awareness of mentalist limits as an excuse for bad action is present in the texts, but it remains an understated background awareness that combines with and underscores the novel's other critiques of Enlightenment thought.

Aggravating this lust to reconnect through persuasion is a counter suspicion of such connectedness to begin with. Cohesion of self with others is simultaneously an object of desire and a matter of foreboding. Unity, of course, in the textbook progressive form of perfection's "chain" is common in the novels to hero and villain alike. *Lovell*'s emphatically good Eduard will cite the "wundersame [...] notwendige Verkettung der Dinge" (274), just as *Abdallah*'s emphatically bad Omar will exalt the "Kette des Erschaffnen" (8). As these parallel but opposed examples suggest, however, the conviction in a unified "chain" of existence is as morally unstable as persuasion is. This instability is more than a matter of Eduard's facile trust in convention (which he has) or Omar's cynical abuse of a commonplace (which he makes) but is also an entailment of unity to begin with.

The problem with unity is that, while it binds and lends purpose to particulars, it paradoxically also strips their sense away. Abdallah's euphoria that "ich schlage an die goldnen Saiten der Natur und verstehe den großen Klang" (46) easily converts to another music metaphor, Omar's vision of the world as "ein Gesang, wo ein Ton den andern verschlingt und vom nächsten verschlungen wird" (5). If musical notes receive their identity from being members of a unified series, they also lose their identity by the same course. As individuals, they exist only to disappear.

As an abstract problem, this liability of the individual to disappearance through unity connects to the grittier generic topic of the novels as novels of persuasion. Like music, persuasion works by combining individual consciences into a general conviction. To persuade is to make two minds coalesce in a harmony of viewpoints. "Nun bin ich dir [...] gleich" says Abdallah at the moment of Omar's persuasion (75), a persuasion that not surprisingly takes place by reawakening Abdallah's memory of the "ganze Harmonie" in his dream of Zulma (51).

In *Abdallah*, Omar's persuasion is as powerful as it is cunning, but he has no announced theory of persuasion; in *Lovell*, Rosa, Omar's counterpart, develops a theory of such personality interchange. The persuader's goal is "sich in die Gesinnungen anderer zu versetzen" (395), so that the persuaded person "ward [...] eine bloße Kopie von mir" (396). Not coincidentally, these remarks appear in a letter to the master persuader Andrea that begins "Deine Meinung ist auch vollkommen die meinige" (395), and they are not idle boasts. Before Rosa even makes these statements, William has acknowledged him as "ein Muster [...], nach dem man sich bilden kann" (324f.). This near science-fiction description of people's "transplanting" into, or "molding" onto, others is clearly ominous: Rosa's letter is a gloatingly melodramatic celebration of having done something bad. The condition, however, noticeably only extends what might otherwise seem a positive "linkage" to others.

William and Rosa are not alone in reaching this dubiously cloned state. William for instance, reaches a similar situation with other figures. Confronting his friend Balder in madness. William acts "aus einem fast unwiderstehlichen Triebe Balders gräßliche Possen nachzuahmen" (652). "Irresistable imitation" becomes a reflex action that William finally projects onto others in his seducer's fantasy when he cannot tell which of his women victims — Emilie, Amalie, or Rosaline — is in his arms (551). These people become as interchangeable as their names (Amalie/Emilie) almost are.

Indeed, these last two woman, whose names sound alike and who are treated as likes treat one another the same way. Emilie writes to Amalie that they "sollen, nur *einen* Busen and *ein* Herz haben," so that Emilie talks "zu Ihnen ganz wie zu mir selbst" (413, emphasis Tieck's). A result is that the letters in the epistolary novel take on an almost antiphonal character, becoming to their readers in the fiction mere echoes of what the readers have already thought or felt. Balder writes William only material that, William says, "ich [...] selbst schon außerordentlich oft gedacht habe" (467); Walter simply "sagt [...] mit andern Worten eben das, was ich soeben behauptet habe" (460).

The unsettling critique of harmony establishes that the early Tieck's novels do not present a voluptuary misunderstanding of Kant but rather connect Kantian ideas directly, and also unsettlingly, to Enlightenment ideas of unity. When people under persuasion come to be other people, they cease to be discrete people; in parallel fashion, the unity of apperception nullifies the individual value of the unified perceptions. As Omar says, our spirit is an "artistically polished mirror that unites scattered and unknowable forms into one ordered picture." In this model of knowing, however, the whole that is knowledge is so only at the total expense of intrinsically distinct, particular objects to know.

The extension of this condition is most noticeable in the novels' familial and political circumstances. Obviously, *Abdallah* and *Lovell* are Oedipal novels, in which sons deliver fathers to death (*Abdallah*) or subject them to psychological torture while destroying their lives' dreams. At heart, the Oedipal situation is one of substitution, in which son replaces father. "Vater, Sohn," says Abdallah, are "nichts als leere Namen," while "father" is "ein blindes Ohngefähr" (180). The cruel final quandary in *Abdallah* is whether the son's perfidious action can win blessedness for the father by achieving the political reforms through the father's death that he would have wanted in life (185). Selim, the father, is in this regard no longer an agent, since his own son is in the godlike role of trying to secure him blessedness. He is an "approximate" whose "name" might as well be someone else's. When the father tells Abdallah to seek "ein besseres Vaterland" (216), he is also telling him to seek a place with more clearly defined, individual terms, where "fathers" can appear as beings distinct from "sons." The Oedipal paradox is, of course, that when the father does function as an agent, the son correspondingly disappears. Much has been made in the critical literature about Walter Lovell's curiously harsh intrusion into William's marriage plans,[10] and the same point could be made about Selim's autocratic attempt to control Abdallah's marital future. As "son" can replace "father," "father" can overwhelm "son." The most harmonious family relation is one in which the individual family member loses significance; himself delivered over to death, Selim sentences Abdallah to die for having made independent marriage plans (174).

The connection of this unhappy harmony to the ideals of the French Revolution is direct. If the revolution comes, as Omar says, from a "Fingerzeig der Gottheit" (38), the principle it represents is a great return to the harmonious equality of all beings. No distinction exists between citizen and king. For all of its surface attractiveness, however, the ontological homogeneity produces more dread than consolation precisely because it verges on a doctrine of identitylessness. Under such conditions, Omar says, "alle Widersprüche vereinten sich [...] in einen Mittelpunkt,[...] keine That gehörte uns, unschuldig kehrten alle zum Schöpfer zurück" (36). When individual conditions are pureed into one common unity, "no action does belong" to anyone in particular.

This is the final horror of Mondal's persuasion, *Abdallah*'s ultimate Masonic demonism. Continuity and perpetuity — otherwise positive doctrines — come to signify that individuals do not belong to themselves. The idea that "wir uns selber angehörten und beherrschten" becomes a wild fantasy (106). As Omar celebrates his final persuasion, he is no longer himself but rather an "unbekanntes [...] Wesen" (240).

Such a suspicion of utterly devaluing particulars through doctrines of harmony comes to inform the novels' most primitive models of language. *Lovell*'s Rosa (395 f.) feels that unity of personalities in persuasion takes place through a kind of sympathetic nonsense language in which the persuader "transplants" himself

---

[10] Walter Münz (supra note 3) has performed the most extensive anaylsis of *Lovell* as a societally very complex Oedipal drama. He is far from the first to notice this feature, however. Robert Minder sees it as a central in *Un poète romantique allemande: Ludwig Tieck* (Paris: Publications de la faculté de l'université de Strasburg, 1936), I, pp. 87 and 92.

emptily into his addressee, an ability made possible because "die Sprache nur in konventionellen Zeichen besteht, und jedermann doch mit dem andern spricht, ob er gleich gut weiß, daß jener durch seine Worte vielleicht keinen Begriff so bekömmt, wie er es wünscht." Such "transplanting" into the addressee through "conventional signs" Rosa then likens to speaking French to the French and Italian to the Italians.

Having established a link through the conventional sign system, Rosa now can pervert individual signs for persuasive purpose: "ich [...] gebe [William] seine eigne Worte anders gewandt ins Ohr zurück." While conventional, this sign system is oddly not durable; the conventionally recognized sign can be "turned" so that it is both traditionally recognizable and not recognizable at the same time. The sign system is also atomistic in that Rosa can change bits of it without affecting other bits of it by leading William to reject "those thoughts" that find no counterpart in his supposed verbal sibling. These bits gone, William "fing [...] emsig einen hingeworfenen Wink von mir auf, und dachte lange über den darin liegenden Sinn." Once discarded, a linguistic "atom" leaves a void behind to be filled by another linguistic "atom."[11] From there the final step in persuasion is taken by the addressees themselves: "sobald man es nur bringen kann, daß sie ihrer gestrigen Empfindung schämen, handeln sie morgens gewiß anders." Vain embarrassment over supposed past error makes the addressee an impassioned defender of his new "linguistic system."

Details of the theory just cited, however, help both explain its failure and illuminate why for Tieck it is an intrinsically disturbing theory. These details are the conflict of "traditional signs" with their interchangeability, and the conflict of the signs' supposed "system" with their atomism.

Rosa's analogy of using "traditional signs" to help persuade — the case of speaking French to the French and Italian to the Italians — has problems at both ends, to which Tieck as prolific translator must certainly have been sensitive. First, Rosa claims his ability to "transplant himself into the addressee" depends on the addressee's recognizing the sign (a French word, say) without recognizing the "concept" (what the speaker means to say). This conception is abstractly understandable if persuasion is taken to mean leading to a hitherto unknown conviction through familiar means, *but* it jibes very oddly with the foreign language analogy. If the speaker says "bon jour" when he mean "de rien," he will certainly not

---

[11] The emptiness of *Lovell* has been often noticed but only rarely tied in to problems of language, as Corkhill remarks (see supra note 8). A rare, earlier counterexample is Horst Lindig's *Der Prosastil Ludwig Tiecks* (Leipzig: n.p., 1937), pp. 11-50. See also: Ernst Ribbat, *Ludwig Tieck: Studien zur Konzeption und Praxis romantischer Poesie* (Kronberg: Athenäum, 1978), pp. 46-64, esp. 49; Thomas Günther Ziegner, *Ludwig Tieck: Studien zur Geselligkeitsproblematik* (Frankfurt a.M.: Peter Lang, 1987) p. 64; Ulrich Scheck, "The Hermetic Self and the Creative Reader: Metanarrative Discourse in Tieck's *William Lovell*," *Seminar* 25 (1989), 96.

establish a bond with the listener but will instead seem to be speaking some species of nonsense. The mere fact of speaking in a foreign language does not mean establishing a meaningful *bond* in a foreign language. To suppose such a bond exists equally supposes the neutral meaninglessness of the language's elements.

The second major problem with Rosa's system as he states and illustrates it concerns the atomistic conception of items in a linguistic system. This is a tenet of great importance in his and Andrea's scheme, at least certainly for realism's sake: in persuading William, a small change in one atom of language is easier to imagine than a quick reshuffling of the entire system. Nevertheless, sudden atomic change violates system to begin with, if the reader accepts Rosa's analogy. If "French" is a system, as Rosa has to believe for his model of transplanting to work, then he would not be able to induce the French to say "bon quack" instead of "bon jour" without effecting many other phonetic and lexical changes across the system. The notion of plucking out one "bit" of language practice and replacing it with another "bit" is at odds with the other belief key to the theory: that the addressee is susceptible to persuasion precisely because all of his beliefs form a compact whole.

If language, like any system, is compact, its parts lose independent significance through having no uniqueness. If it is not compact, its parts equally lose significant through having no intelligible relations to other parts. Tieck's engagement with the radical persuasions of Masonry evidence his early adult awareness of this dilemma as central to his Enlightenment artistic roots.

The irony is that this pessimistic conclusion derives from some of the most optimistic of Enlightenment principles. Nature's chain, the linkage of all into a unity, produces a barrenness of any particulars. Perhaps the prime analogue to this problem is Abdallah's perceptions as he begins the final betrayal of his father. As he dazedly stares "in einzelnen Streifen brach sich der Sonnenschein durch die Fenster und er betrachtete aufmerksam die kleinen zitternden Strahlen, die sich zusammenwebten und wieder auseinanderflogen, sein unverwandtes Auge verlor sich in aufmerksamen Betrachtungen von hundert Kleinigkeiten" (196).

Prismatics — the commonplace symbol of unity — becomes a mere phase state of pointless particularities. In these novels of persuasion, identities coalesce; people come to think with one mind; but in the process they become no more than the "hundred trivialities" of fractured light. Tieck's Enlightenment novels are paradigm Enlightenment novels in following the principle of the prism to it austere conclusion.

INDEX

Adams, Hazard 28, 31
Adorno, Theodor 35, 92
Amrine, Frederick 11
Aner, Karl 37
Aristotle 27, 28, 29, 30, 33, 34, 50
Arnim, Ludwig Achim von 79
Arnold, Heinz Ludwig 25
Atkins, G. Douglas 49
Auer, Karl 70
Baeumer, Max 13
Barker, Frances 17
Barthes, Roland 51, 52
Bate, Walter Jackson 46, 47, 48, 51
Beck, Hamilton 12
Behler, Ernst ix, 108
Benjamin, Jessica 91
Benjamin, Walter x, xi, 95
Benz, Ernst 61
Berdahl, Robert 12
Bertens, Hans 57
Bettelheim, Bruno 91
Biggemann, Friedrich Wilhelm 42
Bloom, Harold 45, 46, 47, 51, 52, 53, 54, 55, 57
Bodmer, Johann Jakob 82
Böhme, Hartmut 8
Böhme, Jakob 58, 59, 65, 67
Bolten, Jürgen 16
Boyne, Roy 81
Brecht, Martin 69
Brecht, Bertolt 14, 77
Bredekamp, Horst 7
Brüggemann, Fritz 105
Büchner, Georg 14, 34
Bürger, Gottfried August 12–21
Burwick, Frederick 9
Cagliostro, Alexander 72
Calinescu, Matei 57
Certeau, Michel de 17

Condillac, Etienne Bonnet de 78
Consentius, Ernst 15
Copleston, Frederick 80
Corkhill, Alan 108, 111
Craig, Charlotte M. 73
Darnton, Robert ix
Daunicht, Richard 20
Derrida, Jacques x, 28, 32, 81
Descartes, René 4, 7, 55, 56, 79
Diderot, Denis 78
Dierauer, Walter 68
Eckermann, Johann Peter 54
Eichberg, Henning 19
Eichner, Hans 105
Elias, Norbert 45–57
Eliot, T.S. 47
Endres, Rudolf 80
Fichte, Johann Gottlieb ix, 3, 7, 70, 72, 107
Fielding, Henry 13
Fink, Gothier-Louis 106
Fischer-Lichte, Erika 13
Foucault, Michel 12, 29, 81, 82
Franz, Gunther 61
Freud, Sigmund 86, 89, 90
Frye, Northrop 47
Gadamer, Hans-Georg 66
Gaier, Ulrich 68
Gassner, Johann Joseph 72
Gay, Peter 78
Gellert, Christian Fürchtegott 80
Gnüg, Hiltrud 15
Göckingk, Leopold Friedrich Günther von 21, 70, 73
Goethe, Johann Wolfgang von 2, 9, 11, 12, 13, 14, 21, 23, 36–44, 45, 54, 55, 56, 57, 68, 70, 77, 79, 83
Gold, Helmut 8
Gottsched, Johann Christoph 81
Grimm, Reinhold 13, 32

Grimm, Jacob and Wilhelm 86–97
Großmann, Sigrid 59
Groth, Friedhelm 60
Gumbrecht, Hans Ulrich 13, 17
Häntzschel, Günter 14, 15, 21
Hardenberg, Georg Philipp Friedrich Freiherr von, see Novalis
Harding, Sandra 27
Hassan, Sally 57
Hassan, Ihab 57
Hayden-Roy, Priscilla 68
Hegel, Georg Friedrich Wilhelm 68, 108
Helvètiusis, Claude Adrien 78
Herder, Johann Gottfried von 14, 29, 30, 32, 41, 68, 70
Hermand, Jost 13
Hinck, Walter 33
Hinderer, Walter 15, 16
Hintikka, Merrill 27
Hippel, Theodor Gottlieb von 80
Hirschmann, Albrecht O. 22
Hoffmann, E.T.A. 42, 98–104
Hoffmeister, Gerhart ix
Höger, Alfons 23
Hölderlin, Friedrich 11, 68
Homer 15
Hörisch, Jochen x
Horkheimer, Max 35, 92
Hume, David 77
Huyssen, Andreas 57
Inbar, Eva Maria 31
Jaeggle, Utz 13
Jäger, Hans-Wolf 75
Jameson, Fredric 31
Jamme, Christoph 8
Jolles, Evelyn B. 14
Joost, Ulrich 18
Kaes, Anton 1, 10
Kaim-Kloock, Lore 14
Kant, Immanuel ix, 27, 28, 31, 34, 38, 61, 68, 70, 72, 74, 75, 77, 80, 82, 83, 84, 108, 109, 110
Kapuscinski, Ryszard 56

Kemp, Wolfgang 13
Kemper, Peter 13
Kermode, Frank 47
Kierkegaard, Søren 46
Kleist, Heinrich von 42
Klinger, Friedrich Maximilian von 42
Klopstock, Friedrich Gottlieb 39
Klotz, Volker 32
Kluge, Alexander 22
Kluge, Gerhart 14
Koopmann, Helmut 16
Korff, August 84
Korzybski, Alfred 50
Krauss, Werner 76
Kühn, Sophie von 9
Kundera, Milan 45, 46, 57
Kurz, Gerhard 8
Kuzniar, Alice 11
La Roche, Sophie von 80
Lacoue-Labarthe, Philippe 32
Lange, Linda 27
Lavater, Johann Kaspar 72
Leibniz, Gottfried Wilhelm 37, 67
Lenz, Jakob Michael Reinhold 14, 19, 20, 27–35
Lessing, Gotthold Ephraim 31, 33, 34, 65, 67, 70, 72, 82
Lewis, Paul 105
Lieske, Rudolf 105
Lillyman, John 107
Lindig, Horst 112
Little, William A. 14, 21,
Llosa, Mario Vargas 49, 50, 57
Locke, John 77
Madland, Helga Stipa 12
Mahal, Günther 36
Mähl, Hans-Joachim 6
Mahoney, Dennis F. 3, 6
Martini, Fritz 32
Marx, Karl 80, 81
Mattenklott, Gert 13, 31
McCarthy John 76, 77
McConachie, Bruce A. 13

McFarland, Thomas 46, 48, 49, 50, 51, 52, 54, 57
Mendelssohn, Moses 82, 84
Mennell, Stephen 45, 47, 50, 55
Merchant, Carolyn 7
Mesmer, Franz Anton ix, 72
Milton, John 39
Minder, Robert 111
Mitcherlich, Alexander and Margarete 95, 96
Möller, Horst 76
Molnár, Géza von 10
Montesquieu, Charles de Secondat 77
Moritz, Karl Philipp 79
Münz, Walter 105, 107, 111
Nägele, Rainer x
Nancy, Jean-Luc 32
Negt, Oskar 22
Neubauer, John 11, 15
Newton, Isaac 9
Nicolai, Christoph Friedrich 70–75
Nietzsche, Friedrich 29, 46, 80, 96, 97
Novalis 1–11, 107
O'Neill, John 12
Ockham, William of 30
Oetinger, Friedrich Christoph 58–69
Outram, Dorinda 12
Philips, F.C.A. 70
Piepmeier, Rainer 64
Pikulik, Lothar 105
Plato 30, 55
Porush, David x
Postlewait, Thomas 13
Prill, Meinhard 68
Promies, Wolfgang 79, 83
Raeff, Marc 13
Rehberg, Karl-Siegbert 45
Rehm, Walther 38
Ribbat, Ernst 112
Richter, Jean Paul 42, 43
Richter, Karl 13
Ritter, Johann Wilhelm x
Rorty, Richard 46, 56

Roskopf, Gustav 37
Rousseau, Jean Jacques 13, 27, 80, 81, 84
Rudwin, Maximilian 36
Russel, Jeffrey Burton 37
Rutschky, Katharina 87
Sabean, David 12
Sachs, Hans 39
Sade, Donatien-Alphonse-François, Marquis de 13
Salumets, Thomas 45
Saul, Nicholas 5
Scarry, Elaine 12
Scheck, Ulrich 112
Schelling, Friedrich Wilhelm Joseph 68
Schiller, Friedrich 4, 12, 13, 14, 15, 16, 17, 21, 42, 70, 76, 84, 85
Schlegel, August Wilhelm 2
Schlegel, Friedrich 2, 8, 9, 70, 105, 107
Schneider, Ferdinand Joseph 106
Schneider, Robert 68
Schneider, Werner 82
Schöne, Albrecht 13
Schönert, Jörg 13
Schubart, Christian Friedrich Daniel 19
Schubert, Gotthilf Heinrich 98, 103, 104
Schulze, Winfried 22
Schummel, Johann Gottlieb 80
Segebrecht, Ursula 13
Semler, Johann Salomo 62
Shaftesbury, Anthony Ashley Cooper, Earl of, 66
Shakespeare 28, 30, 31, 32, 33
Sichelschmidt 71, 72
Siegrist, Christoph 76
Sloterdijk, Peter 14
Snow, C.P. x
Sontag, Susan 57
Sophocles 30
Spieß, Christian Heinrich 76–85
Spindler, Guntram 66
Steiner, George 49
Stevens, Wallace 48
Stiehm, Judith 27

Stierle, Karlheinz 22
Stoppard, Tom 47
Strack, Friedrich 5
Striedter, Juri 4
Strumpell, L. 87
Sulzer, Johann Georg 66
Swedenborg, Emanuel ix, 58, 61, 67, 74
Swift, Jonathan 13, 81
Szondi, Peter 31
Teller, Wilhelm Abraham 58, 61, 62, 63, 66
Thalmann, Marianne 84, 105, 107
Thümmel, August Moritz von 75, 80
Tieck, Ludwig 2, 42, 70, 105–113
Träger, Klaus 76
Trainer, James 107
Trunz, Erich 14
Tymms, Ralph 106
Ueding, Gert 14
Veeser, Aram H. 1
Vico, Giambattista 66
Vigarello, Georges 19
Warncken, Bernd Jürgen 19

Watts, Alan 48, 52
Weber, Samuel 99, 104
Weigand, Karlheinz 106, 107
Weisinger, Kenneth D. 13
Weissberg, Lilian 14
Wellbery, David 64
Wetzels, Walter x, 9
Weyer-Menkhoff, Martin 59
Wieland, Christoph Martin 31, 81
Wiese, Benno von 14
Williams, Bernard 50
Wilson, Daniel W. 107
Wolff, Christian 61, 66, 67, 68, 80
Wüstling, Fritz 105
Zenke, Jürgen 33
Ziegner, Thomas Günther 112
Zimmermann, Rolf Christian 68
Ziolkowski, Theodore 4, 5
Zipes, Jack 92
zur Mühlen, Hermynia 92, 93